The Good Girl Exit

Why Being Good Isn't Working

Kim Black

IngramSpark

Contents

Acknowledgements

There are people without whom this book simply would not exist.

JP, my husband and my person — thank you for never once telling me to tone it down. For usually telling me to turn it up. You are my refuge and the safest place I know.

Flora — you have never once been a Good Girl. You are completely, gloriously feral. I hope you never change.

My girl tribe — the ones who respond to texts that are completely out of context, half-baked, and sent at truly unreasonable hours — thank you for showing up every single time. You know who you are.

The original Sparkle & Soul Collective — you read this first, and you told me the truth. Bold, honest, and exactly what I needed. This book is better because of you.

Tania Carriere of Advivum Journeys — thank you for holding space for my very own Good Girl Exit. Some gifts change everything.

And finally, thanks to Claude *(yeah, that Claude)* for research support, formatting, consistency checks, and copy editing throughout the process. Every source was verified. Every story is real. And mine.

Dedication

For every woman who has been so good, for so long, for everyone else.

Honey, it's your turn.

Introduction

Most women don't wake up one day and decide to disappear.

It happens slowly. Quietly. Over time.

We learn it early, usually without realizing that we're learning anything at all. Through praise and correction. Through what gets rewarded and what gets gently — or not so gently — redirected. Through the small, ordinary moments that teach us how to be acceptable, agreeable, and easy to be around.

We learn how to be good.

Good Girls don't cause trouble. They don't ask for too much. They don't take up space unless there's a clear reason to (and there's usually no "clear" reason) or they've reached their limit and are preparing for a fight.

They learn to enter a room and read it quickly. They notice shifts in tone, body language, and subtle cues. They make quick decisions, almost instinctively, about what will keep things smooth. Over time, carrying the emotional weight of everyone else just becomes normal. It's just part of the package.

Being liked starts to feel safer than being honest. Getting it right feels more rewarded than being real. And without ever consciously agreeing to it, they begin to understand which parts of themselves are welcome — and which ones are better kept quiet.

And for a while, it works.

You get the gold stars. The promotions. The compliments. You build a reputation for being dependable, capable, “so easy to work with.” “The glue” that holds everything together (insert major eye roll here). And it feels pretty good. From the outside, your life may look successful. Impressive, even.

But somewhere along the way, something else starts to happen.

You begin editing yourself before anyone else provides the feedback. You stop asking the questions that you’re curious about and only ask what’s expected. You feel busy and productive — and strangely disconnected at the same time.

You're doing everything "right," and still, something feels off. Not loudly. Not dramatically. Just a quiet, persistent sense that the life you're living has been tailored to fit everyone except you.

This book is about noticing that feeling — and learning to take it seriously.

This isn't a manifesto asking you to burn everything down or reinvent yourself overnight. (Though I'm not opposed to a little disruption.)

It's not about becoming louder, tougher, or more rebellious for the sake of it. And it's definitely not about blaming your past, your parents, your workplace, or yourself.

It's about the small, ordinary ways you learned to leave yourself behind — and what it looks like to come back. Not all at once. Not dramatically. Just honestly.

How to Read This Book

First: there's no right way to do this. (Which, if you're a recovering Good Girl, might be the most disorienting sentence you've read all week.)

Each chapter opens with a short list of statements — not a quiz, not a diagnosis. Just a mirror. If several of them make you feel weirdly called out, that chapter is probably yours. Sit with it.

Inside each chapter, you'll find a story (some mine, some heard, some collective — you'll know which is which), the psychology behind why this pattern made sense in the first place, and moments to pause and actually feel something instead of just reading past it.

At the end of each chapter, you'll get to **Choose Your Exit**:

Quiet — the internal shift. The moment you notice the pattern without feeding it. No announcement, no performance, no one else even has to know. This one's just for you.

Bold — the one you say out loud. The boundary named, the language used, the moment you stop smoothing things over and let the truth take up a little space.

There's no gold star for doing it in order. No prize for finishing fastest. You can read straight through, skip to the chapter that's already making your chest tight, or sit with one page for a week. Dog-ear it. Highlight the parts that feel uncomfortably true. Write in the margins.

This is your book now. Do it your way.

Welcome to The Good Girl Exit

Leaving the Good Girl role doesn't mean throwing her under the bus. She showed up for you. She kept you safe, kept you liked, kept you included when the stakes felt high. She was doing her job — you just get to decide whether she's still the right one for it.

This isn't about burning her down. It's about looking her in the eye and saying: *I've got it from here.*

It doesn't have to be loud. It doesn't have to be dramatic. It doesn't require a resignation letter or a villain or a breakdown — turned — breakthrough moment. Sometimes the exit is a pause before you say yes. Sometimes it's the thing you finally say out loud in a room full of people who expected your silence. Sometimes it's just you, alone, deciding to stop abandoning yourself in small ways you thought no one could see.

(Spoiler: you could see.)

This book will meet you wherever you are — whether you're just starting to feel the itch of something needing to change, or you've been white — knuckling it for years and you're tired of performing a life that stopped fitting a long time ago.

I'm here too, if you want to go deeper. This doesn't have to be a solo journey. But it absolutely can be, if that's what you need right now.

The whisper that brought you to this page? It's not wrong. It's not selfish. And it is — I promise you — never too late.

Stop performing your life. Start living it.

Chapter 1: The Good Girl Who Learns to Play Small

Is This Your Exit?

☐ I walk into a room and immediately start reading everyone else before I've even taken off my coat.

☐ I worry about being "too much" and "not enough" — sometimes in the same conversation.

☐ I've rewritten an email at least three times trying to get the tone right.

☐ I know exactly what my boss, my partner, and my best friend need right now. I couldn't tell you what I need.

If that list felt a little too accurate — keep reading.

What Shrinking Promised

As women, there are so many unspoken rules we contend with across our lives.

Rules about what we should wear. Rules about what we can (and can't) say. Rules about how we should behave. Most of us learned these rules long before we knew we were learning anything at all.

They didn't necessarily arrive as rules. They may not have been rules your parents made you abide by, like get good grades or clean up after yourself.

They arrived as signals.

Be polite. Be pleasant. Don't be too loud. Too emotional. Too opinionated. Smile. Look pretty.

Somewhere between your kindergarten report card and your first real responsibilities, *staying acceptable* stopped being about learning and started being about safety. When you followed the rules — spoken or not — you were rewarded. Maybe it was with approval or a sense of belonging.

And when you didn't, no one needed to yell. The feedback was subtler than that. A raised eyebrow. A gentle correction. A cooling of warmth. Enough that it registered in your brain and subtly taught you how to show up next time.

No one ever hands us a rulebook titled *How to Be a Good Girl*. The rules are sneaky and they come through compliments that come with conditions. Through the difference between "good job" and "maybe next time". They come through watching which girls are celebrated or popular — and which ones are quietly redirected or ignored.

Over time, we just fold. We don't intentionally become The Good Girl, because not everyone was born a Good Girl. But family, career and relationships create the container that requires us to be.

And you've probably, at some point, tried to figure out who you are underneath all of the rules, roles and expectations. But the finish line keeps moving. And you've got laundry to do.

The Haircut

There's a school photo of me that I cannot, to this day, look at without feeling a sense of embarrassment and extreme discomfort. I look at the girl with the wide eyes and the small smile wearing a white Peter Pan collar shirt, and wonder ... what happened to her hair!?

Apparently, my hair was an ongoing battle.

I don't remember this, but my mom tells me it was a mess of knots and tangles. She was constantly after me to brush it, wash it, do something with it, but ... I was 11. And everybody has a grunge phase, right?

One morning, after yet another standoff, my mom had had enough. In a moment of frustration, she grabbed the scissors and chopped it all off.

On picture day.

For her, it was about consequences. It was about minding her. About teaching me a lesson. Cleanliness was essential and how I looked was a direct reflection of her and her parenting abilities. Mind you, this was in the early 80s, and things were a bit different back then. Gentle parenting hadn't yet made it onto the scene and it was more of a do-what-I-say-and-don't-talk-back sort of style.

All I knew is that I was being punished in a way that was devastating. As far back as Bible times, a woman's hair was her crown and glory, so seeing all of mine on the floor and all over the sink is something I remember to this day.

I walked into class that day with hair barely grazing my ears, sticking out in all directions, feeling exposed in a way I didn't yet have words for. And almost immediately, the whispers started.

Why would she do that? Did you see her hair? I wonder what happened.

And those who didn't mind speaking up, spoke directly to me — you look like a boy, you were prettier before.

It stung.

Up until that day, I'd been pretty bold — the girl who didn't mind attention, who took up space without much self-consciousness. But that day, something shifted. I learned that attention could hurt. That difference could and would be mocked.

That haircut became more than a bad style choice immortalized in a school photo. It was the moment I learned that being myself carried risk.

So, I adjusted. And I got smaller.

I tucked the brighter, louder, bolder parts of myself away. Sliding them under what would become a very familiar mask.

The Good Girl.

Why That Made Sense

Children are meaning — makers. But here's what that actually means: we don't sit with an experience and analyze it. We absorb it. We take whatever happened and, almost instantly, turn it into a truth we carry forward — especially when that moment is wrapped up in love, authority, or the fear of losing either.

I didn't walk out of that house on picture day thinking, *that was unfair.*

I walked out thinking I was wrong — and that being wrong could cost me more than I understood at the time.

That's not a dramatic conclusion for a ten-year-old to reach. It's an entirely logical one. Getting small felt like the only safe response to being seen. And from then on, getting it right wasn't just about behavior. It was about staying connected. About not losing access to love, or approval, or the version of myself that other people seemed to prefer.

Layer that with every other message good girls absorb — be agreeable, don't talk back, don't make things harder — and the lesson becomes unmistakable:

If I'm careful enough, I won't lose what matters.

So, you adapt. You edit yourself before anyone asks you to. You soften your edges until you don't recognize them anymore. You comply — not because you're weak, but because you're paying attention. You figured out the rules early, and you've been playing by them ever since.

The problem is nobody told you the game would never end.

When Rules Replace Self-Trust

You're hard — wired from birth for belonging and community. However, you're also hard — wired to keep yourself safe. When the room says you're not safe, you automatically shrink.

You start scanning rooms before you even enter, whether it's through the invite list or your knowledge of the individuals in them. You don't even realize you're doing it. You sense expectations before anyone names them (and many times, this makes you look "proactive", which is always celebrated). You adjust your tone, your timing, your opinions — often before you've checked in with yourself at all.

The habit becomes so practiced it feels like instinct.

From the outside, everything looks fine. Successful, even. You're doing what you're supposed to do. You're building a life, a family, a career ...

But deep inside, something quieter is happening.

You begin trusting the rules more than your own knowing — because the rules feel safer than being seen. You outsource your inner compass. You lose touch with your gut, the version of yourself that existed before "right" became the goal.

Maybe nothing dramatic has happened yet. There hasn't been a big blow up or a breaking point.

It's just a gradual narrowing. And while you fit in with the room, your soul is breaking.

Choose Your Exit

There is absolutely nothing wrong with you. You didn't start shrinking because something was wrong. You learned it because it was rewarded. Because it worked.

The shrinking kept you safe, connected. It helped you to belong.

But you don't have to keep living by rules you learned before you had a choice.

The Quiet Exit

You notice when you're reaching for approval instead of your own truth. You pause — just a beat — before editing yourself. Before softening the thing you were about to say into something more acceptable.

That pause is the exit. It doesn't have to be longer than a breath. It doesn't have to lead anywhere yet.

This isn't about changing everything. It's a slow, soft loosening of the grip.

The Bold Exit

And sometimes, the exit needs a voice.

You name expectations you never agreed to. Allow yourself to change your mind. Stop performing what's expected when honesty would be truer.

It's not rebellion. It's self-trust, spoken out loud.

Chapter 2: The Good Girl Who Mistakes Approval for Belonging

Is This Your Exit?

☐ I'll rearrange my entire schedule before I'd ever ask someone to adjust theirs.

☐ I'm the one who researches the restaurants, books the hotels, and builds the group chat — then wonders why no one does that for me.

☐ I say "sorry to bother you" before asking for something I completely have the right to ask for.

☐ When someone approves of me, I feel loved. When they're disappointed, I feel erased.

If any of that felt embarrassingly familiar — good. That's where we're starting.

What We're Taught About Belonging

The desire for belonging begins the minute we're born. I watch my four-year-old granddaughter seek it with her friends. I chased it in elementary school, playing on the monkey bars when hanging from a rusty bar was the very last thing I wanted to do. I did it as a teenager, begging my mother for the latest clothing trends. And I've done it as an adult, chasing relationships that don't serve me.

Lack of belonging, or loneliness, has been named as an epidemic in our current society.[1] We're all seeking it, yet it seems to be the one thing we just can't get right.

In our quest to belong, we learn to adjust. The lesson arrives quietly and early: Be polite. Use your manners. Don't rock the boat. Don't say too much. Smile.

For girls especially, niceness is often confused with goodness itself. You're praised for being agreeable, for making things easy. You learn to sense the emotional temperature of a room and adjust yourself — your posture, your tone, sometimes your appearance — just to keep the peace.

Over time, you don't just learn how to belong — you learn what belonging requires. Connection becomes something you maintain. Manage. Earn.

Being liked begins to feel suspiciously like being safe.

So you stop asking what am I actually feeling? and start asking what will keep me included? You manage the discomfort by absorbing it. Playing nice stops being a choice and becomes a survival skill.

The Moment I Laughed It Off

I attend a good number of networking events in my role as a solopreneur. Rooms full of people trying to make a living, curiosity about the work I do, and the subtle dance of trying to be impressive without looking like we're trying too hard.

At a recent event, I was standing in a small group when a man made a sexually inappropriate comment about me, to me.

It wasn't loud and it wasn't overt enough to cause a scene, but it was 100% inappropriate.

And it landed hard — right in my solar plexus.

The other people in the group heard it. I know they did. I saw it in their widened eyes. The quick inhale of breath. That collective, unspoken moment where everyone within listening distance thought, *Did he really just say that?*

Now, it's been a minute since I was objectified in that way, so I stood there stunned, caught between disbelief and instinct.

And, in the blink of an eye, I reacted from instinct — I laughed.

Let's be clear. I was NOT okay with the comment. In fact, it continues to sit with me today. I still get a chill when I hear the voice in my head. But, I did what I was taught to do, what I thought I had to do — assess, and quickly triage in order to make it okay for everyone else around me. The quick smile. A light laugh. Me, standing in the crowd, trying not to cry but saying to myself, *It's fine. I'm fine. Let's not make this weird.*

The moment passed and the conversation moved on. No one appeared uncomfortable.

Except for me.

No one spoke up for me in that moment — man or woman. No one checked in with me later to make sure I was okay. And that just reinforces the behavior. Play nice or be excluded.

As a classic over-thinker (do with that what you will), I later replayed it in my head — both the comment and my response to it. The way my body tightened and I literally lost my breath while my face stayed pleasant. The way I swallowed what was true to preserve ease. To protect him. The group. The moment.

Why didn't I speak up? Was the networking really that important to my business? Did I even like the people standing in the group with me? Did I enjoy being there?

I didn't speak up because doing so risked becoming the problem. It risked disrupting the structure already in place. And it risked me no longer belonging.

So I did what I had learned to do well. I swallowed my pride, my psychological safety, my whole being … and played nice.

Why That Made Sense

Playing nice at that moment wasn't a choice. It was muscle memory — my face doing what it had been trained to do while the rest of me quietly went somewhere else entirely.

Our nervous systems are wired to protect belonging. In moments of social tension, the body acts before the brain catches up — scanning not for physical danger, but for relational risk. Will this get me labeled as difficult? Will I lose my place in the group? Will they think I'm overreacting?

That's not weakness. That's a nervous system doing exactly what it was trained to do. The problem is it was never taught another way.

The Story We're Sold

My lack of response wasn't new and it didn't come out of nowhere.

We're taught, again and again, that niceness is the price of connection. As children, it's called being well-behaved. As teenagers, it's not being dramatic. In our careers, it's being professional, easy to work with. In relationships, it's being low maintenance.

Same rule. Different gift wrap.

That's why playing nice shows up in moments so small they rarely make it into stories — the laugh that comes out before you've decided whether something is funny, the email rewritten six times to sound softer, the immediate "yes" that sparks resentment before you even leave the room.

That politeness slowly becomes self-silencing.

When the Need to Belong Becomes Self-Abandonment

Once you see the pattern, it starts showing up everywhere.

My guess is you can come up with two or three ways you've self-silenced just in the past week — even if you consider yourself bold, even if belonging doesn't feel like your thing.

It shows up in the relationship where you became "easy." Where you adjusted your expectations instead of asking for what you need. Where needing less felt like maturity — until the resentment quietly moved in.

It shows up in the role you accepted because you were capable but didn't really want. You're reliable. You're flattered to be asked. Obligation replaced consent.

You stay because leaving risks disconnection. You're quiet because honesty feels dangerous. You accept because belonging doesn't feel like a God-given right — it feels conditional.

And over time, you stop checking in with yourself altogether.

Choose Your Exit

Here's the thing about that moment — and every moment like it: the exit doesn't require the other person to cooperate. This guy wasn't going to change. But I could still choose something different for myself. That's where the agency lives — not in his response, but in mine.

So, I quit the networking group. When people asked why, I explained the situation and they just shook their heads and said, "Yeah, that's just the way he is."

Whether it's my exit or yours, it always begins with a pause.

Nothing too dramatic. Just a moment to ask: What do I actually want here? What would it look like to stay true to myself?

The Quiet Exit

Sometimes, the exit is quiet. Maybe that's just your personality, or you don't feel enough psychological safety to speak up.

You notice the tightening in your chest. The reflex to smile when there's nothing in particular to smile about. The urge to smooth the moment so everyone else can stay comfortable.

Instead of jumping into the fray, wait. Stay silent. Let the discomfort belong to the person who created it. And remind yourself: *I don't need to manage this.*

Sometimes the quiet exit is enough to change the tone of the individual/group/room and you've instantly regained your agency in real time.

The Bold Exit

And sometimes, the exit is spoken.

"That comment doesn't sit right with me."
"I'm not comfortable with that."
"What would make you say something like that?"

No lecture. Just a clean line drawn in the sand of your truth.

People will squirm. They may apologize. Some will move on and ignore you completely.

What matters is that you stood for yourself.

Chapter 3: The Good Girl Who Hustles for Her Worth

Is This Your Exit?

☐ I feel guilty doing nothing — even when doing nothing is exactly what I planned.

☐ I was the first to put my hand in the air and volunteer — then regretted it immediately.

☐ I've pushed through sick, through grief, through burnout — because stopping felt more dangerous than continuing.

☐ I can tell you every open loop on the team's project list, in the house, in the relationship. I couldn't tell you the last time someone asked what I needed.

Feel that in your gut? Keep reading.

What Hustle Promised Us

There's a particular kind of exhaustion that doesn't feel like exhaustion at first.

It feels like purpose.

You're the one who shows up early and stays late. The one who anticipates what the room needs before the room knows it needs anything. You manage the task *and* the people *and* the unspoken logistics — and you do it well enough that no one questions the cost. Least of all you.

For many Good Girls, productivity isn't just a habit. It's a form of protection.

If I'm useful, I'm safe. If I'm indispensable, I am seen. If I'm the hardest worker in the room, no one can question whether or not I deserve to be here.

The hustle starts young. Gold stars. Honor rolls. Being the kid who finishes first *and* helps the kid next to her. It gets reinforced in our careers — the woman who's "always available," who "never drops the ball," who somehow keeps it all running while also being pleasant about it (and looking pretty while doing it).

We don't just do the work. We carry the mental load — the work around the work. The pizza ordering. The note-taking. The emotional temperature checks. The invisible labor that keeps teams functional and people comfortable.

And that translates into our home lives, as well. We'll talk later about ordering toilet paper ... and if I need to say more, this may not be your chapter.

But because we're competent, more gets added. Because we don't complain, more is assumed. The bar doesn't stay where it is — it rises. Quietly. Constantly. And we rise to meet it, because that's what we've always done.

Until we no longer can.

The Flight Home from St. Louis

I was deep in my road warrior season. The kind of consulting life where you fly out on Sunday or Monday and don't come home until Friday afternoon. Week after week. City after city.

On this particular trip, I was doing what I always did — leading the project, keeping the group on task, managing timelines, literally chasing people down hallways to make sure deadlines were being met. I was the project manager in the room.

But I was also the one ordering the food. Taking the notes. Grabbing office supplies. In a room full of mostly men, those tasks had somehow become mine — not because anyone formally assigned them, but because I volunteered. Because I always volunteered. Because if something needed doing and no one else was stepping up, I filled the gap. That's what Good Girls do.

By day three, my body started sending signals. A sniffle. A heaviness settling into my bones. That creeping, rundown feeling that whispers *slow down* while everything around you shouts *keep going*.

I kept going.

By the end of the week, I boarded my flight home with a searing earache. The pressure was so intense, so relentless, that I cried the entire flight from St. Louis to Houston. Not quietly. Not the polite kind of tears you can blink away. The kind that doesn't care who's watching — because the pain had overridden everything else.

When I finally landed and made it to the airport parking garage, I sat in my car and couldn't remember how to turn it on.

Not in a metaphorical way. Not in an "I was so tired I could barely think" kind of way, but. I sat there, staring at the dashboard, and genuinely could not recall the sequence of steps to start my own car. My body had been running on fumes for so long that my brain had simply stopped cooperating.

After a trip to the ER, I learned I had a severe ear infection. The doctor told me I could have burst my eardrums — that I risked losing my hearing, temporarily or permanently — because I'd flown with that level of pressure and infection.

Because I pushed through.

Because I always pushed through.

Why That Made Sense

We don't push ourselves to the point of collapse because we're careless. We do it because the system rewards it.

And if you're a woman in a room full of men, the stakes are different. You're not just doing the job. You're justifying your presence in it. Every time. So you absorb the logistics, run the meeting, keep everything moving — and make it look effortless, because effortlessness is what everyone has come to depend on from you.

It's a heavy suit of armor. And armor is exhausting to wear every single day.

The Backslide

I took a week off to recover. And when I came back, something had shifted. Not all the way — not a full Good Girl Exit — but enough to matter. I started drawing small boundaries around my health and safety. I stopped being the first to volunteer for every invisible task. I paid attention when my body spoke up, instead of overriding the signal with willpower.

But here's the thing about the Good Girl pattern: it doesn't leave quickly or quietly. Years and years of conditioning is tough to break through.

Not long after the ear incident, I found myself on another project in Denver. The project was due on Monday, so I assumed everyone would stay the weekend to finish it up. Wrong. The rest of the team started disappearing on Friday afternoon. No commentary, no explanation. They were just gone, done for the week. They all packed up and flew home.

No one informed me.

I sat in my hotel room, alone while the rest of the team was at home with their families. And I was missing my kids' weekend activities. Missing time with my husband. Sitting in a city I hadn't chosen to be in, wondering how I'd ended up here — again.

Denver is a great city. I found things to do. I made the best of it.

But that quiet hotel room became a loud speaker.

The hustle hadn't just cost me my hearing (almost). It had cost me weekends. Presence. The parts of my life that actually mattered.

So I stepped back into my exit. I opened my laptop and started looking for new jobs.

And then I left.

The Story We're Sold

Our culture loves a woman who hustles.

She's a go-getter. She's driven. She's "the glue" that holds the team together. (Insert eye roll here.)

We celebrate overwork as ambition. We reward burnout as dedication, as an expectation. We hand women the invisible labor — the emotional maintenance, the logistical management, the keeping-everyone-comfortable work — and then praise them for being "team players" when they absorb it without complaint.

Choose Your Exit

You didn't learn to hustle because something was wrong with you. You learned it because it worked — until it didn't. Until your body broke down in a parking garage, or you woke up in a city that wasn't yours, or you realized you'd been running so hard you forgot to check whether you were even running toward something you wanted.

The exit doesn't require you to stop being excellent.

It requires you to stop using excellence as proof that you matter.

The Quiet Exit

You notice the urge to volunteer before anyone else does. The reflexive "I'll handle it" that comes before you've even checked whether you want to. The guilt that rises when you sit still for too long.

Instead of acting on it, you pause. You ask yourself: *Am I doing this because I want to — or because I'm afraid of what it means if I don't?*

You let the silence sit. You let someone else fill the gap. You allow yourself to be in the room without earning your place in it.

The Bold Exit

And sometimes the exit has teeth.

"I can manage the project or I can order lunch. I'm not available to do both."

"I need to leave on time this week (and don't apologize for it)."

"I've been volunteering quite a bit lately, and I'd like us to start rotating the responsibility."

No performance. No justification. Just a clear, steady reclaiming of your time and energy.

People may be surprised. Some may push back. A few might not even notice — because the work you've been carrying was invisible to begin with.

But you'll notice.

And that's enough.

Chapter 4: The Good Girl Who Has to Earn Her Rest

Is This Your Exit?

☐ I feel guilty sitting down when there's still something on the list — and there's always something on the list.

☐ When someone else takes over, I spend the whole time watching to see if they're doing it right. (They're not.)

☐ I watch other people take breaks freely and feel genuinely confused by them.

☐ My body has started making the decision for me — headaches, insomnia, getting sick the minute vacation starts — because I won't.

Consider this your permission to sit down. You don't have to earn this chapter.

What Rest Was Supposed to Be

Rest should be simple.

You're tired, so you stop. You're depleted, so you replenish. Your body says *enough*, and you listen.

But for many women, rest doesn't work that way. Rest isn't a response to exhaustion — it's a reward. Something you get *after*. After the house is clean. After the lunches are packed. After everyone else has what they need. After you've proven, beyond any reasonable doubt, that you've done enough to deserve a moment of stillness.

The problem, of course, is that the *after* never comes.

There's always another load of laundry. Another email. Another permission slip. Another human being who needs something from you before you're allowed to need something for yourself.

And so rest gets pushed. Delayed. Shrunk down to the last twenty minutes before sleep, which you spend scrolling through your phone because your nervous system has forgotten how to actually wind down. And PS — doomscrolling or sitting in bed with your iPad only makes it worse.[3]

We don't withhold rest from ourselves because we're martyrs. We do it because we were taught — early and repeatedly — that rest is for people who've finished. And women, particularly mothers, are never finished.

Lauren

Lauren couldn't tell you the last time she sat down without a reason.

Not a real sit-down. Not the kind where your body actually releases and your mind goes quiet and you exist, briefly, without an agenda.

When she did stop — when the kids were finally in bed and the kitchen was close enough to clean and there was nothing left that absolutely had to happen tonight — she'd sink into the couch and immediately reach for her phone. Not because she wanted to. But because stillness felt wrong. Uncomfortable in a way she couldn't quite name. Like waiting for something to go sideways.

She'd scroll. Check the school app. Add three things to tomorrow's list that she'd thought of while pretending to watch TV. Text her sister back. Check the school app again.

An hour later, she'd drag herself to bed — more tired than when she sat down, and somehow no more rested.

She didn't think of this as a problem. She thought of it as just how things were. Rest, real rest, was for later. For when things calmed down. For when she'd done enough to deserve it.

The thing no one told her — the thing she was only beginning to suspect — was that later wasn't coming. And "done enough" wasn't a finish line. It was a moving target she'd been chasing her whole life.

Why That Made Sense

Lauren's inability to rest wasn't a personality quirk. It was logic.

When your value has always come from what you produce — from how much you give, how smoothly you keep everything running — then stopping isn't rest. It's a threat. The machine goes quiet. And if the machine goes quiet, everything you've built your identity around goes quiet with it.

The cage is so normalized most women can't see the bars. And the cruelest part? After enough years, we lock it ourselves.

The Guilt Loop

Here's how the cycle works, and if you recognize it, you're not alone:

You push until you're depleted. Your body sends a signal — a headache, a cold, an ache that won't leave, nights of insomnia that have you dragging yourself out of bed because you're not sure you even closed your eyes. You ignore it because there are lunches to pack and deadlines to meet and a child who needs you to hold the world together.

Eventually, something forces the stop. Illness. Injury. A breaking point you never saw coming.

You rest — but only because you have no choice. And even then, the guilt is immediate. You feel lazy. You feel like you're failing. You hear the voice that says *other women handle this without complaining.*

So the moment you feel even slightly better, you're back. Full speed. Overcompensating for the pause. Proving that the rest didn't mean you're weak.

The guilt isn't a flaw. It's the enforcement of years of Good Girl conditioning. It's the invisible draw that keeps you in the cycle, ensuring that rest never lasts long enough to actually change anything.

Choose Your Exit

Lauren didn't need permission to rest. She needed to stop believing she hadn't earned it yet. And so do you.

Rest isn't a reward for finishing. It's a requirement for continuing. And the guilt you feel when you take it? That's not your conscience. That's the conditioning.

The Quiet Exit

You stop negotiating with yourself about whether you've done enough to deserve a pause.

You notice the guilt when it rises — and you let it be there without obeying it. You sit down before the list is done. You let someone else handle bedtime. You let the dishes sit in the sink and you don't narrate an apology in your head while they do.

The quiet exit is the moment you stop earning your rest and simply take it.

The Bold Exit

And sometimes the exit requires a conversation.

"I need Saturday mornings. Not as a favor — as a standing plan."

"I'm not going to check in while I'm gone. I trust you to handle it."

"We need to talk about how rest is distributed in this house, because right now, it's not equal."

No guilt. No over-explaining.

Rest isn't something your partner grants you. It's something you reclaim — not from them, but from the belief that you don't deserve it unless every box is checked and every person is tended to.

Chapter 5: The Good Girl Who Takes On What Isn't Hers

Is This Your Exit?

☐ I carry a running mental list that exists entirely in my head and nowhere else.

☐ I've written detailed instructions for things other adults should already know how to handle — and I wasn't even asked.

☐ I've been called "the glue" at home, at work, in friendships — and honestly? I'm tired of being sticky.

☐ If I stopped tracking and reminding, things would fall apart. I know this because I tested it once and I was right.

If you're mentally listing everything that needs to happen after you finish this chapter — this one's for you.

The Work Before the Work

There's a kind of labor that doesn't look like labor.

It doesn't show up on a to-do list. It doesn't get assigned in a meeting. It doesn't have a job title or a line item or a performance review. It lives in the background — constant, invisible, and almost entirely carried by women.

It's knowing that the toilet paper is running low before anyone else notices. It's tracking which kid has soccer on Tuesday and which one has a project due Thursday. It's remembering that the credit card bill auto — pays on the fifteenth but the water bill doesn't, so someone has to manually log in, and that someone is always you.

It's not the doing. It's the knowing that it needs to be done.

Researchers call it cognitive labor, or the mental load.[4] It's the project management layer of life — the planning, tracking, anticipating, and remembering that keeps a household or a team or an entire office running. And it's exhausting in a way that's difficult to articulate, because from the outside, it doesn't look like you're doing anything at all.

You're not scrubbing the floor. You're noticing the floor needs scrubbing, adding it to the list, figuring out when it can happen, and making sure the cleaning supplies aren't running low — all while cooking dinner and answering an email from your kid's teacher.

The mental load isn't a task. It's a thousand tasks that live inside your head at all times, running like software in the background, consuming energy you can't account for and no one thinks to ask about.

Rachel

Rachel couldn't remember the last time she'd been sick enough to actually stop.

Not the kind of sick where you push through with cold meds and a brave face. The kind of sick where your body makes the decision for you. The real kind — fever, chills, the whole-body ache that turns your bones into something achy and unfamiliar. The kind that pins you to the bed and doesn't negotiate.

For three days, Rachel did almost nothing. She slept. She drank water when she remembered. She let the house run on whatever momentum her usual systems had built — the lunches she'd prepped earlier that week, the calendar reminders she'd already set, the grocery list she kept on her phone that no one else ever looked at.

Her husband handled the kids. He made dinners (of a sort). He got them to school (mostly on time). He checked homework (or at least asked whether it was done). He was present and trying, and she was grateful for that, even through the fog of a 102-degree fever.

But he didn't check the toilet paper.

Why would he? He'd never been the one who tracked it. He'd never opened the hall closet, glanced at the shelf, and made a mental calculation — *four rolls left, family of five, that's about three days, add it to the list.* That math had always happened inside Rachel's head, silently, automatically, alongside a hundred other calculations just like it.

So on day three of the flu, from underneath a pile of blankets, Rachel heard it.

A voice from upstairs. One of the kids. Loud, indignant, and unmistakable:

"THERE'S NO MORE TOILET PAPER!"

Not *we're running low.* Not *where do we keep the extra?*

There's no more. None. In the entire house.

Because the one person who tracked it — who always tracked it, who tracked everything — had been horizontal with a fever for 72 hours. And in her absence, nobody else in the house had even thought to look.

Rachel lay there, sick and exhausted, and almost laughed. Almost.

Because there it was. The entire mental load, illustrated by a single missing household item. Not a crisis. Not a catastrophe. Just toilet paper. And yet it revealed everything — every invisible system she'd built, every quiet calculation she ran without being asked, every piece of the household infrastructure that lived exclusively in her head and nowhere else.

If she stopped, the toilet paper ran out.

Imagine what else would unravel if she stopped for longer.

The Mental Load Doesn't Stay Home

If the mental load only lived within the walls of Rachel's house, it might have been manageable. Frustrating, but contained. Something she could compartmentalize, address on weekends, negotiate with her partner over time.

But it doesn't stay home. It follows you to work.

There, Rachel carried a different version of the same invisible weight. She was, officially, a project manager but the role had quietly expanded to include things that were never in the job description.

She tracked deadlines no one else remembered. She noticed when the printer was low on toner and ordered more before anyone had to ask. She kept a mental catalog of who was behind on what, which meetings were likely to run over, and which team members needed a nudge versus a direct conversation. She remembered birthdays. She organized the lunch order when clients visited. She knew where the extra phone chargers were kept.

No one assigned her these tasks. No one asked. She just ... did them. Because she noticed, and because no one else seemed to, and because if she didn't, they wouldn't get done. Or they'd get done poorly. Or they'd get done late, and she'd end up fixing it anyway.

Her competence became her trap.

The more capable she proved herself, the more was assumed. The more she absorbed, the more invisible the labor became. Her team didn't thank her for tracking the things they forgot — because they didn't know she was doing it. It was seamless. Effortless-looking. The way it always is when someone is doing the work so well that the work itself disappears.

She was the operating system, and everyone else just used the apps.

Why This Made Sense

The mental load doesn't land on women by accident. It lands there by design — and the design starts early.

She tracks because no one else does. No one else does because she always has. She can't stop because the one time she did, the toilet paper ran out and a child was stranded on the toilet yelling about it.

The cycle doesn't need anyone's permission to continue. It just needs her to keep showing up.

The Real Weight

Here's what makes the mental load so insidious: it's not any single task. It's the *accumulation.*

It's not that tracking toilet paper is hard. It's that tracking toilet paper is one of 300 things you're tracking simultaneously, and no one else is tracking any of them, and the moment you stop — even for something as legitimate as the flu — the system fails.

The weight isn't in the doing. It's in the never being able to stop thinking about the doing.

It's lying in bed with a fever, and somewhere in the back of your burning, aching brain, a small voice whispers: *Did anyone move the laundry to the dryer?*

That voice doesn't take sick days. It doesn't clock out. It doesn't get weekends. It runs constantly, quietly, and it is exhausting — not because any one thought is heavy, but because the thoughts never stop.

Choose Your Exit

The mental load isn't yours because you're better at it. It's yours because you picked it up and no one ever reached for it.

Putting it down doesn't mean things fall apart. It means other people learn to notice — the same way you did. Because it's necessary.

The Quiet Exit

You stop preempting. You notice the impulse to add something to the list, to remind, to track — and you let it sit. You let the toilet paper run low. You let someone else discover the gap and figure out how to fill it (and maybe squirrel away an emergency roll for yourself).

You resist the urge to swoop in when the system stutters. There will be snafus. Just remind yourself: *This is not my failure. This is the redistribution of responsibility.*

It will feel uncomfortable. Things might slip. The discomfort is not evidence that you should take it back. It's evidence that you were carrying too much.

The Bold Exit

And sometimes the invisible has to be made visible before it can be shared.

"I need to show you something. This is everything I'm tracking right now — at home, at work, in my head. I need you to see it."

"I'm not the only person in this house who can notice when we're running low on something."

"I've been managing things at work that aren't in my job description, and I'd like to talk about how we redistribute them."

You don't have to carry it all to be valuable. You don't have to be the operating system. You're allowed to close some tabs.

Chapter 6: The Good Girl Who Carries Everyone Else's Feelings

---

Is This Your Exit?

☐ I can feel the mood of a room the second I walk in — and I've already started adjusting before I've said hello.

☐ I'm the person everyone calls to vent — and I rarely say no, even when I'm already running on empty.

☐ People describe me as "so calm under pressure." They have no idea.

☐ I hold it together so consistently that no one ever thinks to ask if I'm okay.

If you read that list and immediately thought about someone else who needs to read it — honey, it's you.

The Invisible Skill

Some women carry feelings the way other women carry handbags — constantly, automatically, and so naturally that no one notices the weight.

It starts as a skill. A matter of sensitivity. The ability to read a room, sense a shift in tone, feel the emotional temperature drop before anyone else registers the change. As girls, it's praised. *She's so empathetic. She's such a good listener. She always knows when something's wrong.*

What no one tells you is that the skill has a cost. And the cost compounds over time.

Because once you become the person who notices, you become the person who manages. You absorb the tension so others don't have to sit in it. You soften your response so someone else's reaction doesn't escalate. You hold space — for your partner, your kids, your coworkers, your mother- in-law, your clients, the stranger at the coffee shop who just needed someone to listen — and you do it with a steady voice and a calm face and teeth clenched so tight your dentist has started asking questions.

The world sees composure. Your jaw tells a different story.

The Year Everyone Needed Me

I'm a coach. Holding space is literally my job.

I'm trained for it. I'm good at it. I know how to sit with someone in their pain without trying to fix it, mostly without absorbing it, without letting it consume me. I know the techniques. I teach the techniques.

And then COVID happened.

In the span of a few weeks, the world cracked open and totally shut down. People lost their jobs, their routines, their sense of safety. Loved ones were dying. Fear was everywhere — thick and ambient, like humidity you couldn't escape.

My clients showed up on Teams calls from their bathrooms — because their roommate or their partner was working in the only other available room. They showed up from closets. From parked cars. From kitchen counters shared with their children's Zoom classrooms. They showed up frightened and grieving and angry and lost, and I held space for every single one of them.

That was my job. I did it well. I stayed calm. I stayed present. I stayed steady.

And then I closed my laptop, left my office, and walked downstairs.

Where my mother-in-law was waiting.

She had moved in with us — or rather, she had settled in, the way some people do, gradually and then completely. She was needy in a way that consumed every molecule of air in the room. Every conversation orbited her anxiety, her discomfort, her complaints. She took advantage of my availability and my inability to say no — because I was the one who held space. That's what I did. For everyone.

So I held space for her.

And then my youngest daughter needed me. The world had stopped, and she was frustrated — she had things to do, places to be, a life that was supposed to be moving forward, and instead she was stuck inside, watching the walls close in. She needed patience and reassurance and someone to absorb the unfairness of it all.

So I held space for her.

And then my husband, who couldn't travel for the first time in years, who was learning to work from home, who was adjusting to a version of daily life he'd never had to navigate before — he needed room to figure it out. Room to be frustrated. Room to feel displaced in his own home.

So I held space for him.

Clients during the day. Mother- in-law in the afternoon. Daughter in the evening. Husband at night. Sometimes overlapping, but never slowing down.

I absorbed every frustration, every anger, every sadness.

And I held my body so tightly through all of it that my teeth began to crack.

Not a metaphor. My dentist looked at the x-rays and told me I'd been grinding so hard, so constantly, that the structural integrity of my molars and my front teeth were compromised. My jaw was doing what my mouth wouldn't — clenching against everything I refused to say, bracing against the weight I refused to put down.

People at work still called me "calm under pressure."

I was calm the way a bridge is calm — holding the weight of everything crossing it while the infrastructure quietly fractures underneath.

The Parking Lot

I had a nervous breakdown.

I want to say that plainly, because I spent a long time not saying it at all. I softened it. I called it burnout. I called it "a rough season." I told people I'd been "going through some things." I used every euphemism available to avoid the truth, because the truth felt like failure — especially for a woman whose entire career was built on helping other people hold it together.

But the truth is, I broke.

I was driving to my therapist's office — a session I'd had on the books for weeks. I remember getting in the car. I remember pulling out of the driveway.

I don't remember anything after that.

The next thing I knew, I was in the parking lot. Engine running. Hands on the wheel. No memory of the drive — the turns, the lights, the other cars on the road. Fifteen minutes of my life simply gone. I had dissociated. My nervous system, after months of absorbing everyone else's pain while ignoring my own, had simply checked out. Left the building. Shut down everything nonessential just to keep the body moving forward.

I sat there, shaking.

Not the subtle kind. The kind that starts deep — somewhere behind your ribs — and radiates outward until your hands can't grip the steering wheel and your legs aren't sure they'll hold you upright. My body was giving out — not from illness, not from exertion, but from the sheer accumulated weight of every feeling I'd held for every person who needed me to be okay.

I barely made it into the office.

That session was the beginning of treatment. Real treatment — not the kind where you talk about your week and get coping strategies and go home feeling slightly lighter. The kind where you admit that the foundation has cracked and you can't patch it anymore. The kind where a professional looks at you and says, in so many words, *You cannot keep living like this.*

I tell you this not because I owe you my story, but because I know — I *know* — there's a woman reading this who is holding everything for everyone and her teeth are cracking and her jaw is locked and her face is calm and she thinks she's fine.

You are not fine. And that's not a failure. It's a signal.

If the woman who does this for a living couldn't outrun it, neither can you. And you shouldn't have to.

Why That Made Sense

Women are trained to be emotional first responders — an actual job we were handed before we were old enough to know we'd accepted it.

The skill gets reinforced because it works. Every time you hold space for someone else, you get rewarded. With trust. With closeness. With the quiet validation of being the one people turn to.

But nobody teaches you how to put it down. Nobody teaches you that empathy without a limit isn't generosity — it's self-erasure. That being everyone's safe place means you don't have one.

You didn't take this on because you're soft. You took it on because you were rewarded every single time you did — and nobody told you there was another option.

Choose Your Exit

You don't have to stop being empathetic. You don't have to stop caring. You don't have to become cold or guarded or unavailable.

You just have to stop being the only one who holds.

The Quiet Exit

You notice when someone else's feelings start living in your body. The tightness in your chest that isn't yours. The heaviness after a conversation that was about someone else's problem. The clenching jaw that shows up every evening like clockwork.

Instead of absorbing, you observe. You let the feeling exist in the room without pulling it into your body. You remind yourself: *I can care about this without carrying it.*

You let someone's bad mood belong to them. You stop adjusting yourself to regulate someone else's experience. You unclench your jaw — literally — and notice what it feels like to let go.

The Bold Exit

And sometimes the exit means saying the thing out loud.

"I love you, and I can't be your only outlet for this."

"I need someone to ask me how I'm doing — and actually wait for the real answer."

"I've been holding a lot for a long time, and I need help. Not the kind I can give myself."

No one will offer to carry what they can't see. And for too long, you've made the carrying look effortless.

Let them see the weight. Let them see the cost. Let them see you — not the composed version, not the steady version — the real one. The one whose teeth are cracking.

That version of you deserves to be held, too.

Chapter 7: The Good Girl Who Mistook Beauty for Worth

Is This Your Exit?

☐ I've spent money I didn't really have on products or procedures to fix something I was told was a flaw.

☐ I feel less valuable — not just less attractive, but actually less worthy — when I don't look put together.

☐ I've caught myself comparing my face or body to women 10 or 20 years younger and feeling like I'm already losing.

☐ I know the beauty standard is a lie. I also spent 45 minutes on my appearance this morning.

If you laughed at that last one — and then felt a little sad — this chapter belongs to you.

The First Currency

Before you could read, before you could write your own name, you understood one thing about being a girl: pretty mattered.

It arrived before language. In the way adults lit up when you wore a dress. In the way "sit pretty" was offered not as fashion advice but as behavioral instruction — a way of being, not just a way of looking. In the compliments that always seemed to land on appearance first and everything else second. *What a pretty girl. Look at those curls. Aren't you adorable?*

No one told you that your face was your resume. They didn't have to. You absorbed it the way children absorb everything — through repetition, through reward, through the subtle mathematics of what earns attention and what doesn't.

By the time you reached adolescence, the learning had expanded. The teenage years added a sharper edge. Magazines told you what was wrong with your body before you'd finished growing into it. Mean girls ranked each other by appearance with surgical precision. Boys made comments that landed like verdicts — about your weight, your skin, your chest, your hair — and you learned, quickly, which ones opened doors and which ones got you dismissed.

You weren't just learning how to be attractive. You were learning that attractiveness was a form of safety and belonging. That being pretty bought you patience, attention, and inclusion. That being ugly — or even just average — was a kind of social risk.

And so you invested. Not because you were vain. Because you were paying attention.

Diane

Diane was the kind of woman people called "put together."

She had a system. A morning routine that took 45 minutes, minimum — moisturizer, serum, primer, foundation, concealer, blush, brows, lashes. A closet organized by season and occasion. A rotation of highlights, lowlights, and trims every six to eight weeks. A standing appointment for facials every month.

In her twenties, the maintenance felt fun. Playful. An expression of who she was. She liked experimenting with lipstick, trying new looks, feeling polished. She loved the attention it got her.

In her thirties, it shifted. Subtly at first. The products got more targeted. Eye cream. Retinol. SPF every single day, rain or shine. The compliments started coming with qualifiers — *you look amazing for your age* — and she wasn't even forty yet.

By her forties, the maintenance had become management. She was no longer enhancing something she liked. She was fighting something she feared. The fine lines around her eyes. The shifting texture of her skin. The way her jawline had softened. The single gray hair that multiplied into twenty before she could decide how she felt about them.

The products multiplied too. Serums with peptides. Creams with hyaluronic acid. A vitamin C step. A retinoid step. An eye cream that cost more per ounce than anything in her refrigerator. A separate neck cream, because apparently the neck needed its own product now.

And then came the procedures.

It started with Botox. Just a little. Just the forehead, just to "soften" the lines that showed up in every Zoom call. Then filler — just a touch, just to restore what time had quietly taken. Then the consultations about lasers, chemical peels, microneedling. Each one presented not as vanity but as self-care. *You're investing in yourself. You deserve to feel confident.*

Diane tracked her spending once, out of morbid curiosity. Products, procedures, appointments, supplements. The number startled her. She was spending thousands of dollars a year — not on travel, not on education, not on experiences — on the maintenance of a face and body that the world had taught her was her most important asset.

And the thing that sat with her most? It was never enough. There was always a new concern, a new product, a new procedure promising to fix the thing the last one didn't quite reach. The finish line kept moving — because there was no finish line. The entire industry was built on making sure you never arrived. And never felt comfortable in your skin — whatever your age.

The Silver Fox Problem

Around the same time Diane was investing in her third serum and debating whether she was "a Botox person," her husband turned fifty.

He'd gone gray at the temples. His face had lines — real ones, the deep kind. He'd gained weight in the way middle-aged men do, softly and without apology.

And people told him he looked great.

Not great for his age. Just great. Distinguished. Like a silver fox. Like he was finally growing into his face.

No one suggested he try a serum. No one told him his neck needed attention. No one pulled him aside at a dinner party and whispered the name of a "wonderful dermatologist." No one looked at his crow's feet and saw a problem to be solved.

He was aging. And the world received it as evidence of character.

Diane was aging, too. And the world received it as a decline to be managed.

The same gray hair that made him "distinguished" made her "letting herself go." The same wrinkles that gave him "gravitas" gave her "a tired look." The same decade of living had written itself on both of their faces — and only one of them was expected to erase it.

That's not a beauty standard. That's a tax. One levied almost exclusively on women, collected by an industry that generates nearly $677 billion a year globally[5] — an industry built, in large part, on the premise that women's faces and bodies are problems to be solved, maintained, and optimized until the day they die.

The anti-aging market alone is valued at nearly $78 billion, with women accounting for nearly 70% of all purchases.[6] Millennials are starting anti-aging routines at 26 — two full decades earlier than the generation before them.[7]

The message has been received. Start early, fight hard, never stop. And somehow, it still won't be enough.

Why That Made Sense

Here's the maddening part: the investment in beauty isn't irrational. That's what makes it so hard to walk away from.

The research is real. Attractive people — as defined by whoever's setting the cultural norms at the moment — are perceived as more competent, more trustworthy, more likable. They get hired more often. They earn more. They're given the benefit of the doubt in rooms where other people have to fight for credibility.[8]

For women, the stakes are even higher, because beauty was never just correlated with social advantage — it was sold to us as the *path* to it. Be pretty and you'll be liked. Be desirable and you'll be chosen. Stay youthful and you'll stay relevant.

That's the bargain. And most of us accepted it before we were old enough to read the fine print.

The fine print, of course, is brutal: the bargain expires. Beauty as currency has a shelf life, and the market decides when yours is up. Which means the thing you were told would protect you — the thing you spent years curating and maintaining and spending thousands of dollars to preserve — was always going to run out.

You weren't vain. You were playing the game you were handed. The problem was never you. It was always the game.

The Cost Behind the Counter

Let's talk about what Diane's "self-care" actually cost. Not just financially — though the financial toll is real. The average American woman spends more than $200,000 in a lifetime on beauty products and services.[9] Over a lifetime, that's a house. A retirement fund. A business.

But the deeper cost is psychological.

It's the morning spent staring at your face in a magnifying mirror, cataloging flaws that no one else would notice at normal distance.

It's the photo you deleted because the angle caught your jawline wrong. It's the event you almost didn't attend because nothing in the closet made you feel like the version of yourself you think you're supposed to be.

It's the quiet math you run every time you enter a room — am I the youngest? The thinnest? The most put-together? — and the way your confidence shifts based on the answer.

It's the realization, somewhere in your forties or fifties, that you've spent more time maintaining your appearance than developing any other part of yourself. Not because you're shallow. Because prettiness was the skill that always got a return — until it didn't.

And when it stops working — when the compliments thin out, when the attention shifts to the younger woman in the room, when the world begins treating you as invisible — what's left?

That's the question the beauty industry never wants you to ask. Because if you sit with it long enough, you might stop buying.

Choose Your Exit

You don't have to throw out every product in your bathroom. You don't have to stop caring about how you look. Enjoying beauty — color, style, self-expression — isn't the problem.

The problem is when beauty becomes proof. When looking good is the only way you know how to feel worthy.

The Quiet Exit

You notice the voice. The one that says *you look tired* and means *you're not enough.* The one that tallies your flaws before you've finished your coffee. The one that tells you the gray hair needs fixing before anyone sees it.

You let the voice talk. And then you don't obey it.

You leave the house without the full routine and notice that the world doesn't collapse. You let the gray come in — for a week, a month, or forever — and see what happens when you stop fighting your own face. You look in the mirror and practice the radical act of not finding a problem.

The Bold Exit

And sometimes the exit is spoken — to yourself, to your daughter, to the culture at large.

"I'm done spending money on the fear of aging."

"I'm not going to apologize for looking my age."

"You can call him distinguished. You can call me distinguished too."

The bold exit isn't about rejecting beauty. It's about refusing to let it be the primary measure of your worth. It's about deciding that your face — your real face, the one with lines and texture and evidence of every year you've lived — is not a problem to be solved.

It's about looking in the mirror and seeing someone who's *lived* — and deciding that's more than enough.

Chapter 8: The Good Girl Who Learned to Disappear

Is This Your Exit?

☐ I've dressed for other people's comfort more often than my own expression.

☐ I've looked in the mirror and not recognized the woman looking back — not because of age, but because she's been curated by someone else's preferences.

☐ I struggle to answer, "what do you want?" in a restaurant, in a relationship, in my own life — because I stopped asking myself a long time ago.

☐ There are parts of me I buried so long ago I'm not sure I'd recognize them if they came back.

If that last one stung a little — good. She's still in there.

The Art of Vanishing

Some women disappear loudly. A dramatic exit. A door slammed. A life upended.

Most women disappear the other way.

Quietly. Gradually. One small concession at a time. A preference surrendered here. An opinion swallowed there. A closet that slowly stops reflecting who you are and starts reflecting who someone else wants you to be.

The disappearing doesn't feel like disappearing while it's happening. It feels like adapting. Like compromise. Like love, even — the willingness to bend yourself toward another person's shape because the alternative feels like rejection.

You don't wake up one morning and decide to erase yourself. You do it the way you learned to do everything else as a good girl — by reading the room, sensing what's wanted, and quietly becoming it.

Until one day you look around and realize you've become so good at being what everyone else needs that you've lost track of what you actually are.

Megan

Megan was 16 when she fell in love for the first time.

He was everything she thought she wanted — confident, popular, the kind of boy who made you feel chosen. His family was close-knit, traditional, put together in a way that felt warm and stable. His mother wore Laura Ashley — soft florals, lace collars, modest hemlines. His sister dressed the same way. They were a matching set of femininity that looked, to Megan, like belonging.

Megan was not Laura Ashley.

She was bold colors. Trendy cuts. The girl who experimented with style because clothing was one of the few places she felt like herself. She liked being noticed — not in a desperate way, but in a way that said *I'm here, and I chose this.*

But being with him meant fitting in with his world. So she adjusted. She traded the bold colors for florals. The edgy cuts for modest lines. She started dressing like his mother and sister — not because anyone sat her down and told her to, but because it made sense toher: look like them, be accepted by him.

It felt like a costume. She knew it did. But she told herself it was the price of being wanted. A small sacrifice. A worthwhile trade.

She wore the costume for two years. And then he left for college, and she was cast aside — quietly, efficiently, the way boys that age discard whatever no longer serves them.

She was heartbroken. And still, she was wearing someone else's clothes.

The Next Disappearing

What Megan did next is what many women do after a loss: she jumped.

Straight from one relationship into another. Straight from one set of expectations into a new one — only this time, the expectations weren't subtle.

Her first husband was explicit.

He told her what to wear. Clothes he didn't approve of disappeared from the closet — not metaphorically. They were gone. Removed. As if they'd never existed. He was vocal about how she looked, what was acceptable, what wasn't. The message wasn't coded or subtle. It was direct: *You will look the way I want you to look.*

If the Laura Ashley period was a costume she chose to put on, this was a uniform she was ordered to wear. And she did it, because it meant being accepted.

Megan covered herself. Head to toe. Not because she wanted to, but because the cost of being visible — of wearing something he didn't sanction, of expressing something he didn't approve of — was worse than the slow, suffocating act of vanishing inside a blouse or a skirt that wasn't her choice.

For almost two years, she lived inside that disappearance. Two years of dressing for his approval, speaking in tones he found acceptable, shrinking herself into a shape that fit inside his control.

And then — quietly, without the drama the moment deserved — she left.

She was twenty-something years old. She found the strength to start over. And she had absolutely no idea who she was or how to figure it out.

The Void After

Leaving was the brave part. What came after was the disorienting part.

Megan stood in front of her closet — what was left of it — and felt nothing. No instinct. No pull toward any particular color or cut or style. The part of her that once knew how to dress herself, how to show up in the world as *herself*, had gone quiet. Not because it was gone. Because it had been overwritten — first by a boyfriend's family aesthetic, then by a husband's control — so many times that the original signal had been buried under years of someone else's preferences.

She didn't know what she liked anymore. Not just in clothing — in anything. Restaurant menus were paralyzing. Decisions felt dangerous. The question: *what do you want?* — a question most people answer without thinking — sent her into a spiral of uncertainty and anxiety.

Because wanting things had never been safe. Wanting things meant risking disapproval. Wanting things meant being visible. And being visible, in her experience, meant being corrected, controlled, or abandoned.

So she'd learned to not want. Or at least to not know what she wanted. Which, over time, amounts to the same thing.

The Silence You Wear to Bed

There's another kind of disappearing that lives in this chapter. One that's harder to talk about — because we were taught, explicitly, not to.

Sex.

For many Good Girls, the disappearing doesn't stop at the closet. It follows you into the most intimate space of your life — and it operates there with a silence so complete that most women don't even recognize it as a pattern.

Megan grew up in a home where sex wasn't discussed. Not in a vague, we'll-get-to-it-later way. In a way that was heavy with implication. The message, delivered through religion and culture and the wordless weight of what was never said, was unmistakable: sex was shameful. Desire was ugly. Good girls didn't think about it, didn't ask about it, and certainly didn't want it.

So Megan arrived at her first sexual relationship knowing almost nothing about her own body. She didn't know what she liked — because she'd never been given permission to find out. She didn't know what to ask for — because asking implied wanting, and wanting implied something about her character that she'd been taught to fear.

So she performed.

She performed the way good girls perform everything — by reading the room, sensing what was expected, and delivering it. She faked what she didn't feel. She prioritized his experience over hers. She treated intimacy like another space where her job was to make someone else comfortable — and her own pleasure, her own experience, her own body's honest response was irrelevant. Or worse — embarrassing. Not ladylike. Too much.

This is what silence breeds. Not just ignorance about anatomy or technique — but a fundamental disconnection from desire itself. When no one teaches you that your body is yours, that your pleasure matters, that wanting is allowed — you don't just miss information. You miss *yourself*. You become a ghost in your own bed.

And for many women, that haunting lasts years. Decades. An entire adult life built on the assumption that intimacy is something you give, not something you experience.

The Discovery

Here's what no one tells you about the disappearing: the way back isn't a straight line, and it doesn't happen in the places you'd expect.

For Megan, it didn't start in a closet. It didn't start with a makeover or a bold outfit or a dramatic reinvention. It started in a room full of strangers, at a writing workshop.

She'd enrolled in the workshop as a way to improve her writing skills, something she had always loved to do, a way to build something of her own after years of building herself around other people. But the workshop didn't just teach her how to coach others. It turned the mirror around.

It asked her to look at her own stories. The roles she'd been playing. The expectations she'd been living inside. The narratives she'd absorbed — about who she was, what she deserved, how she should show up — that had been running her life like invisible software.

And for the first time, she started unraveling them.

Not all at once. Not neatly. But thread by thread — each role examined, each expectation questioned, each story held up to the light and asked: *Is this mine? Or did someone hand this to me?*

The clothes came back first. Slowly. A color she hadn't worn in years. A cut that felt like *her* instead of like someone else's idea of her. The kind of choices that seem small from the outside but feel enormous when you've spent a decade letting other people dress you.

And then — later, more quietly — the other reclamation. The one that happened in private. The slow, tender discovery that her body had opinions. That desire wasn't shameful. That pleasure wasn't something she owed to someone else — it was something that belonged to her. That she was allowed to want, to explore, to feel, to ask, to know herself in the most intimate way possible — not as a performance, but as an experience.

Megan didn't become a different person. She became the person she'd been before the costume, before the control, before the silence. The one who liked bold colors and wasn't afraid to take up space.

She'd been in there the whole time. Waiting. Under all those layers of someone else's preferences.

She just needed permission to come back.

And then she realized: she never needed permission at all.

Why That Made Sense

Women don't disappear because they're weak. They disappear because the world makes visibility expensive.

Being fully seen means being judged. Being expressive means being corrected. Being sexual means being labeled. Being loud means being too much. Being yourself — completely, unapologetically yourself — means risking the one thing Good Girls are taught to protect at all costs: belonging.

So you dim. You adjust. You blend in. You dress for his comfort, his mother's approval, the office's unspoken dress code. You wear what makes you palatable. You perform in relationships. You stop asking what you want because wanting has always been a liability.

Each small act of disappearing is a rational response to an irrational set of expectations. You didn't choose erasure. You chose safety. And for a long time, they looked like the same thing.

They were never the same thing.

The Story We're Sold

Our culture romanticizes the disappearing woman.

She's "low maintenance." She's "easygoing." She's "not one of those women who makes everything about herself." She's the cool girl, the supportive wife, the team player, the woman who doesn't need much and never asks for more.

We celebrate her adaptability without asking what it cost. We praise her agreeableness without wondering what she swallowed to get there. We reward her invisibility and call it maturity.

And in the most private spaces — in the bedroom, in the body — the silence is even more complete. Women's pleasure is still treated as optional or embarrassing. A woman who knows what she wants sexually is still, in many circles, viewed with suspicion, with judgment. A woman who doesn't is never questioned at all.

That silence isn't accidental. It's structural. And it starts long before the bedroom — in the homes where sex was never discussed, in the churches where desire was sinful, in the culture that taught generations of girls that their bodies existed for other people's purposes.

The disappearing doesn't start with a controlling partner or a bad relationship. It starts with a world that never taught you that being visible — fully, physically, sexually, loudly visible — was your right.

Choose Your Exit

You didn't disappear because something was wrong with you. You disappeared because you were taught that visibility was dangerous — and you were smart enough to believe it.

But you're not sixteen anymore. You're not in that relationship. You're not wearing that costume.

And the woman underneath all of it — the one with bold taste and strong opinions and a body that has things to say — she's still there.

The Quiet Exit

You start with one choice. One thing that's just for you.

A color you haven't worn in years. A preference you name out loud — at a restaurant, in a meeting, in your own home. A moment where you resist the urge to ask "what do you think?" and instead sit with what *you* think.

You ask yourself one honest question: What do I actually want here? Not what's expected. Not what's easiest. Just what's true. You don't have to answer it out loud. You just have to stop not asking.

Nobody needs to notice. You will. And that's the point.

The Bold Exit

And sometimes the exit is a full reclamation.

"I'm done dressing for anyone else's comfort."

"I want to talk about what I want — in this relationship, in this bed, in this life."

"I've spent years being invisible, and I'm not doing it anymore."

You don't owe anyone an explanation for becoming visible again.

You don't need to justify why you suddenly have opinions, preferences, desires. You don't need permission to exist in full color.

You just need to stop waiting for someone else to tell you it's okay to be seen.

It's okay.

It was always okay.

Chapter 9: The Good Girl Who Waits to Be Chosen

Is This Your Exit?

☐ I've told myself I'll go after the thing when I'm "ready" — and that day hasn't arrived.

☐ I ask for feedback not because I need direction, but because I need someone to tell me it's okay to proceed.

☐ I've watched someone less qualified get the opportunity I was waiting to be offered.

☐ The question "who am I outside of this role?" terrifies me — mostly because I don't have a quick answer.

Still waiting for a sign? This is it. Keep reading.

The Line That Never Moves

There's a particular kind of waiting that Good Girls specialize in.

It doesn't look like waiting. It looks like patience. Like humility. Like "not wanting to be pushy." Like knowing your turn will come if you just keep showing up, keep doing the work, keep being excellent and agreeable and easy to overlook.

We wait for the promotion. For the invitation. For the relationship to be offered. For the mentor to say *you're ready*. For the audience to appear before we create the thing. For some external signal — a credential, a compliment, a cosmic permission slip — that tells us it's okay to step forward and claim what we've been circling for years.

We wait because Good Girls don't grab. Good Girls get chosen.

Yet again, we were taught this early. Raise your hand and wait to be called on. Don't be bossy. Don't be too ambitious. Let it come to you. If you're good enough, the right people will notice.

And so we wait. We prepare endlessly. We refine, revise, and research. We tell ourselves we need one more certification, one more year of experience, one more piece of evidence that we've earned the right to take up space.

Meanwhile, the line never moves. Because the line was never real. It was just the distance between who you are and who you're willing to let yourself become — maintained by the belief that someone else has to close the gap for you.

No one is coming to choose you.

Not because you're not worthy. But because the choosing was always yours to do.

The Empty Calendar

I know this because I lived it.

For 25 years, I had a career. A title. A calendar so full it defined my days, my weeks, my identity. I was the woman who had somewhere to be, something to manage, a role to fill. I was competent and visible and needed. I showed up early, stayed late, and built a professional life I was certain I'd retire from.

And then it was gone.

Not gradually. Not on my terms. Just — gone. The job I'd given a quarter of a century to decided it was done with me before I was done with it.

I woke up the next morning and stared at my calendar.

Nothing.

Not a meeting. Not a deadline. Not a single place I was expected to be. The entire day stretched out in front of me — empty, open, and absolutely terrifying.

From the outside, it probably looked like freedom. A fresh start. An opportunity to reinvent. People said things like *This is exciting! Think of the possibilities!* And I smiled, because that's what Good Girls do when the world falls out from under them — they smile and pretend the freefall feels like flying.

But here's what was actually happening: I was standing in the middle of my life without the one thing that had told me who I was for 25 years. And without it, I didn't know.

I thought I did. Everyone thought I did. I was the woman with the career, the coaching practice, the energy, the confidence. I knew who I was.

Except I didn't. I knew what I *did*. I knew the role. I knew the performance. I knew the version of myself that showed up when there was a calendar to fill and a title to carry. But the woman underneath all of that — the one who existed without a role to play, without a room to manage, without a task to prove her worth — I hadn't checked in with her in decades.

The job loss didn't create the identity crisis. It revealed one that had been there all along, humming beneath the surface like static — noisy enough to feel like a soundtrack, until the music stopped and I realized the static was all there was.

The Worth Question

Here's what I discovered in that silence: I didn't know what I was worth without something to show for it. A huge portion of my worth was wrapped up in my work identity. And that makes sense — as we spend more than 90,000 hours of our life at work.[10]

Not in a dramatic, existential way. In the quiet, practical way that shapes every decision you make without announcing itself. My worth had been tied to productivity for so long — to output, to usefulness, to the evidence of a full calendar and a busy life — that without it, I felt like I'd been subtracted from my own equation.

And the voice that showed up wasn't Who are you now?

It was: *Does anyone care?*

That voice wasn't new. I recognized her immediately. She'd been waiting in the wings every time I'd considered writing, creating, building something that was mine instead of someone else's. She asked the same questions every time:

Will anyone care about this? Am I wasting my time? Who am I to think I have something worth saying?

These aren't questions about quality. They aren't market research. They are questions about permission — the Good Girl asking whether anyone has officially sanctioned this, whether she's been chosen for it, whether there's enough external validation to justify taking up this much space.

The answer, of course, is that the permission was never coming. It's never going to come. The validation is not a prerequisite. It is a fantasy we use to delay doing the thing we're afraid to do.

So I stopped waiting for it. And I wrote the book.

The Book You're Holding

This book — the one in your hands right now — is my exit.

It didn't come easily. It came with 10 years of stopping-and-starting writing my first book. The starts and stops had nothing to do with writer's block, but something more honest — *worth* block. The belief that choosing my own voice, my own framework, my own story required validation before it counted. If someone would care.

It came with the loss of a job that stripped away the identity I'd been hiding behind. With the terrifying blankness of a calendar that had nothing on it. With the slow, uncomfortable reckoning of asking *who am I when I'm not being useful to someone else?*

It came with JP — my partner, my constant — who listened to every idea, crazy or otherwise, and never once told me to tone it down. Who usually told me to dial it up. Who came out of retirement so I could have the space to create and dream.

It came with my coaching practice — with sitting across from women who were stuck in the exact same patterns I was stuck in, telling them to choose themselves, to trust their own voices, to stop waiting for permission — and then closing my laptop and realizing I wasn't walking my talk.

It came with the realization that I only knew a part of myself. That the static I'd been hearing for years — the noise of roles and expectations and other people's definitions of me — had become my whole playlist. And the only way to hear something different was to get quiet enough to find it.

So, I took some time. I asked myself some tough questions. And I wrote this book.

Not because someone chose me. Not because an agent called or a publisher knocked or the universe sent a sign written in the sky.

I wrote it because I chose myself.

And that — choosing yourself without proof that anyone else will — is the hardest, and most rewarding, exit in this book.

Why We Wait

Waiting is what happens when you've spent a lifetime being told that stepping forward uninvited is the same thing as overstepping. It's the logical result of a lifetime spent being told that good things come to those who wait — to those who earn, who prepare, who demonstrate enough value to be selected.

Men are taught to apply for the job when they meet 60% of the qualifications. Women wait until they meet 100%. That statistic has been quoted so often it's become a cliché — and it turns out, it might not even be a statistic. Researchers traced it back to an offhand comment made by a Hewlett-Packard executive, not a study. No data. No methodology. Just a remark that felt true enough to travel.[11]

And yet — the behavior it describes is real. Harvard Business School researchers found that when equally qualified men and women were shown the same job posting, just 6% of qualified women applied for the advanced position. Twenty-two percent of men did.[12]

The cliché was wrong about the numbers. It was right about everything else.

The gap isn't about confidence. It's about conditioning. Good Girls are trained to be chosen, not to choose. To be discovered, not to declare. To wait for the external validation that says *now you're ready* — because the internal knowing was never treated as enough.

And so we wait. For the tap on the shoulder. For the sign. For the feeling of readiness that never quite arrives — because readiness, for a Good Girl, is just another word for *someone else said it was okay.*

Meanwhile, the thing you've been waiting to do — the book, the business, the conversation, the life — sits in the corner of your mind, gathering dust and urgency in equal measure.

It's still there. It's been waiting for you the way you've been waiting for permission.

The difference is: it can't choose you. Only you can choose it.

Choose Your Exit

You've been waiting long enough.

Not because you're impatient. Because the thing you've been waiting for — the permission, the validation, the certainty — isn't coming. Not from a boss, not from a partner, not from a credential, not from the market.

The only person who can choose you for the thing you most want to do is you.

The Quiet Exit

You stop waiting for the feeling of readiness and start anyway. You notice the voice that says *who are you to do this?* and you answer it: *I'm the one who's here.*

You open the document. You make the call. You sign up. You begin — not when it feels safe, but while it still feels scary. Because the scary feeling isn't a sign that you're not ready. It's a sign that this matters.

The Bold Exit

And sometimes the exit is a declaration.

"I'm not waiting for permission anymore."

"I'm starting this — not when I feel ready, but now."

"I've been waiting for someone to tell me I'm qualified to live my own life. I'm done waiting."

No one needs to choose you first. No one needs to validate your path before you walk it. No one needs to tell you that your voice matters before you use it.

You are the authority on your own life. Choose accordingly.

Chapter 10: The Good Girl Who Was Never Taught How to Be Angry

---

Is This Your Exit?

☐ I wasn't allowed to express strong feelings growing up, so I got very good at feeling nothing. Or looking like it.

☐ I've been called "cold" or “difficult" the moment I stopped being agreeable. Interesting.

☐ I swallow what I'm actually feeling — and it shows up later as exhaustion, anxiety, or a very specific kind of resentment.

☐ I've described myself as "fine" so many times I've almost forgotten what not-fine feels like.

If reading that made you feel something you can't quite name — that might be the point.

The Forbidden Feeling

Every Good Girl has go-to emotional vocabulary. She has access to "pleasant", "fine", "steady", "easy", "agreeable". She can walk into a room and make every single person in it feel comfortable — because her own comfort was never on the list of things that needed managing.

But the big feelings? The ones that take up space, that make noise, that require other people to do some adjusting of their own?

Those were off — limits. Not just anger. All of it.

Stop getting so emotional. Why are you crying? I'll give you something to cry about.

Some women learned to reroute anger into tears — because tears were at least tolerated. But for others, the tears got shut down, too. Crying was a weakness. Crying was inconvenient. Crying was something other people couldn't deal with, so you learned not to do it.

Which left you with nothing. No acceptable outlet for anger. No acceptable outlet for grief. No outward channel at all. Just the standing mandate: be pleasant, be steady, and under no circumstances make anyone in the room deal with your feelings.

So the feelings didn't leave. They went underground. Into your jaw. Into your shoulders. Into the 3 AM thoughts that won't stop circling. Into the resentment you can't quite name but can always feel. Into the anxiety that showed up the moment you stopped moving long enough for it to catch you.

Your anger didn't disappear. It just learned to wear different outfits. And it has been waiting, patiently, for you to finally let it speak.

Nadia

Everyone liked Nadia.

That was the first thing people said about her. Not that she was smart — though she was. Not that she was talented — though she was that, too. *She's so warm. She's so easy to be around. She makes everyone feel comfortable.*

Nadia had been warm her entire life. It was her currency. The thing that opened doors, smoothed rooms, held relationships together. She was the one who remembered birthdays, who checked in after hard conversations, who made the new person on the team feel welcome, who laughed at jokes that weren't funny because the alternative felt like a social risk she couldn't afford.

Warmth wasn't a personality trait. It was a survival strategy. One she'd been running since childhood.

Her mother didn't tolerate big emotions. Not anger. Not tears. Not anything that disrupted the household's careful equilibrium. The rules weren't posted on the refrigerator. They were delivered in tone — sharp, swift, and effective.

Stop it. You're being dramatic. I'll give you something to cry about.

Nadia learned early that feelings — the real kind, the messy kind — were a problem to be solved, not an experience to be felt. She learned to read her mother's face the way other children read picture books — constantly scanning for shifts in mood and tone, adjusting her own reactions accordingly. If her mother was tense, Nadia was quiet. If her mother was frustrated, Nadia was helpful. If her mother was angry, Nadia was invisible.

She never questioned why her mother operated that way. She didn't need to. Children don't analyze their parents' patterns. They absorb them. And whatever had taught her mother to clamp down on emotions — whatever had come before, in her mother's own childhood, her own training, her own silencing — had been passed down without explanation. Just the rule, delivered clean: *We don't do that here.*

By the time Nadia was an adult, she didn't just suppress emotions. She'd stopped recognizing them. The wiring that converts sensation into feeling and feeling into expression had been so thoroughly dismantled that she genuinely couldn't tell you what she felt in any given moment — beyond "fine." Beyond "good." Beyond the pleasant, steady hum of a woman who had learned, decades ago, that the safest feeling was no feeling at all.

The Day She Stopped

It wasn't a breaking point. There was no catalyst. No single event she could point to and say *that's when everything changed.*

One Tuesday morning, Nadia simply stopped.

She stopped softening her emails with cute exclamation points and smiley face emojis. She stopped offering to take notes in meetings. She stopped laughing at her boss's jokes. She stopped asking her husband how his day was before he asked about hers. She stopped filling silences with warmth just because empty air made other people fidget.

She didn't yell. She didn't confront. She didn't slam a door or write a manifesto or make a scene.

She just stopped performing.

And the response was immediate.

“Is everything okay? You seem … off.”

“You've been really quiet lately. Are you sure nothing's wrong?”

“I don't know, she's just been kind of cold.”

Cold.

Not angry. Not frustrated. Not someone who might have a reason for the shift. *Cold.* As if the absence of her warmth was a weather event — an unexplained temperature drop in a room that had grown accustomed to her heat.

No one asked what she was feeling. No one asked what she might be angry about. Because that would have required them to consider that her warmth had never been free — that it had been labor, performed daily, at a cost that nobody thought to calculate because nobody thought to ask.

They didn't want to know why she was angry. They wanted her to stop being cold. They wanted the warmth back. They wanted *their* Nadia back — the one who made them comfortable. The one who managed the room so they didn't have to manage themselves.

The label wasn't a diagnosis. It was a demand: *Go back to who you were. We preferred it.*

Where It All Went

Here's the thing about an emotion that has no exit: it doesn't dissolve. It migrates and festers.

Nadia didn't think of herself as an angry person. She didn't think of herself as a sad person, either. She was a *steady* person. Someone who was capable, who handled things.

But the evidence was everywhere — if you knew where to look.

It was in the resentment she carried toward her husband — the slow, quiet kind that doesn't announce itself but poisons everything it touches. Years of absorbing more than her share, saying *it's fine* when it wasn't, watching him move through life with a freedom she couldn't name or claim. She wasn't angry at him. She was angry at the arrangement — and at herself for agreeing to it.

It was at work, where she'd spent years being passed over, talked over, and credited under. Where she'd watched men with half her experience and a fraction of her competence take seats she'd earned — and she'd congratulated them, because that's what warm people do. The anger lived in every email she rewrote to sound softer, every idea she let someone else present, every performance review that praised her teamwork without ever mentioning her leadership.

It was in the way crisis always found her — not to fall apart in, but to manage. When her father got sick, the family organized itself the way families do around a capable woman — without anyone deciding to, without anyone asking. Her mother fell apart. Her sister fell apart. And Nadia made the calls. She researched the options, coordinated the hospice intake, followed up on test results, updated the family group chat with the facts everyone needed and no one wanted. She held the logistics so that everyone else could hold their feelings.

No one asked if she was okay. Not because they didn't love her. Because she was handling it — and handling it meant she didn't need to be held. Her competence had become permission for everyone else to feel while she managed. And somewhere in that season, the grief went underground too, joining everything else she'd been storing for decades.

It was in her body. The migraines that arrived every Sunday evening like clockwork, right as the weekend's stillness made room for whatever she'd been outrunning all week. The insomnia that wasn't really insomnia — it was a mind with nowhere to put what it was carrying, spinning the same thoughts at 3 AM because the daylight hours were fully booked with performances and responsibilities.

It was in the over-functioning — the compulsive need to control every detail of the household, the calendar, the workflow. Not because she was a perfectionist. Because controlling the external world was the only safe way to manage the internal pressure. If everything around her was in order, she didn't have to face the disorder inside.

And underneath all of it — beneath the resentment, the workplace injustice, the physical symptoms, the control — was the deepest layer.

Anger at herself.

For how long she'd let it go. For how thoroughly she'd participated in her own suppression. For every "fine" that was a lie, every pleasant smile that cost her something, every moment she chose someone else's comfort over her own truth. She wasn't just angry at the world for teaching her to shut down. She was angry at herself for being such an excellent student.

That anger — the self-directed kind — is the hardest to sit with. Because it doesn't have a villain. It doesn't have a clear target. It just has you, looking at the years behind you, wondering what might have been different if someone — anyone — had taught you that feelings were allowed.

Why She Was Never Taught

Girls are taught to manage emotions. Boys are taught to have them.

That's an oversimplification — but not by much. The research is consistent: from early childhood, girls are socialized to prioritize relational harmony. They're praised for being kind, for sharing, for including, for de-escalating.[13] When a girl gets angry, the response is usually swift — *use your words, calm down, that's not nice, don't make a scene.*

When a boy gets angry, the response is different. Often it's tolerated. Sometimes it's encouraged. It's reframed as passion, competitiveness, or as evidence of a strong will.

But for girls like Nadia — girls raised in homes where *all* emotional expression was treated as a disruption — the training goes deeper than gender socialization. It becomes neurological.[14] The nervous system learns, through repetition, that feeling leads to punishment. Not physical punishment, necessarily — though sometimes that too. But the withdrawal of safety. The cooling of the room. The threat implicit in *I'll give you something to cry about* — which teaches a child not just to stop crying, but to stop feeling the thing that caused the tears in the first place.

That training gets passed down. Not always intentionally. Mothers who were silenced often silence their daughters — not out of cruelty, but out of an unconscious belief that suppression is protection. *If I teach her not to feel too much, the world won't hurt her the way it hurt me.*

It's a devastating kind of love. The kind that protects you by erasing you.

And when a woman raised inside that silence finally does express something — anything, even the mere absence of warmth — the labels arrive so fast they function as a warning to every other woman watching.

She's aggressive. She's emotional. She's cold. She's difficult to work with. What happened to her? She used to be so nice.

The labels aren't descriptions. They're corrections. They say: *Get back in line. We didn't give you permission to feel this.*

They return to the version of themselves that feels safer — the one that doesn't make anyone uncomfortable.

Nadia almost did. She felt the pull — the instinct to soften, to reassure everyone that she was still the same pleasant woman they'd always known. The pull was ancient. It lived in her nervous system, right next to the voice of her mother.

But this time, she didn't go back.

The Reclamation of Anger

Here's what Nadia learned when she stopped going back:

Anger isn't the opposite of warmth. It's the companion to it. You can't feel deeply in one direction without the capacity to feel deeply in the opposite direction. The same sensitivity that makes you attuned to other people's feelings is the same sensitivity that registers when something is wrong, unjust, or unbearable.

Anger is yet another signal. It's your nervous system telling you that a boundary has been crossed, a value has been violated, a part of you has been ignored for too long. It's not the problem. It's the body's way of pointing to the problem.

And the women who've been told their whole lives not to feel it? They're not lacking anger. They're drowning in it. It's in their jaws and their shoulders and their racing thoughts and their snapped responses and their resentment and their exhaustion and their control.

Anger was never the enemy. The silence around it was.

For Nadia, it didn't happen the way she expected. There was no breakthrough conversation. No cathartic confrontation. No moment of clarity in a therapist's office.

It happened on a Tuesday night. Two glasses of wine. An episode of American Idol she'd seen before. Nothing special. Nothing designed to crack her open.

But her nervous system, for the first time in longer than she could remember, finally felt safe enough to let go. And the tears came — not the controlled kind, the tidy kind she could explain away — but the full-body kind. The kind that shook her shoulders and wouldn't be reasoned with. The kind that had been waiting, apparently, for exactly this level of ordinary.

She cried for a long time. She wasn't entirely sure what she was crying about. All of it, maybe. The years of "fine." The grief she'd managed instead of felt. The anger she'd swallowed so many times it had become part of her diet.

When it was over, she felt something she didn't have a word for at first. Not happiness. Not relief, exactly. Just — space. Like a room that had been cleared of furniture she'd stopped noticing was there.

She poured the rest of the wine. Kept watching. Let the credits roll.

That was all. That was enough.

And the tears? The ones that were shut down alongside the anger? Those were never weakness either. They were the body's other language — the one that says *this matters to me, this hurts, I am a person who feels things* — and they were taken away too. Not because they were dangerous. Because they were inconvenient.

Feeling isn't a flaw. It's proof that you're alive. And the woman who reclaims her anger — who lets it exist without renaming it, without softening it, without apologizing for the discomfort it causes — isn't losing her warmth.

She's discovering that warmth, without honesty underneath it, was never real warmth at all.

Choose Your Exit

You were never taught how to be angry. You were never taught how to cry without consequence. You were taught that the only safe emotion was pleasantness — and you've been living inside that lie ever since.

This is your permission to stop.

The Quiet Exit

You name it — to yourself. In your body, in your journal, in the quiet of your own mind. You stop translating your feelings into something more palatable. You stop calling it stress when it's anger. You stop calling it anxiety when it's grief. You stop calling it "nothing" when it's everything.

The next time you feel the heat rise — the tightening, the clenching, the flash of *this isn't right* — you don't smooth. You don't redirect. You don't perform.

You sit with it. You let it be anger. You let it be sadness. You let it be whatever it actually is, without editing it for someone else's comfort.

That's not cold. That's the warmest thing you've ever done for yourself.

The Bold Exit

And sometimes the feeling needs a voice.

"I'm angry about this. And I'm not going to pretend I'm not."

"I've been called cold because I stopped being warm. That's not my problem to fix."

"I was taught that my feelings were an inconvenience. I'm unlearning that now, and it might be uncomfortable for both of us."

People will be uncomfortable. They'll want the old version of you — the warm one, the easy one, the one who made the room feel good.

Let them be uncomfortable. You've been uncomfortable for years. It's their turn now.

Anger, expressed cleanly and without apology, isn't aggression. It isn't coldness. It isn't a character flaw.

It's the sound of a woman who finally stopped swallowing her own fire.

And the tears, when they come — and they will come, because the dam can't hold forever — aren't weakness.

They're thawing.

Chapter 11: The Good Girl Who Thinks Confidence Comes Later

Is This Your Exit?

☐ I deflect compliments like they're incoming fire. ("Oh, this? It was nothing.")

☐ I over-prepare, over-research, and over-qualify — because I don't fully trust myself to just know something.

☐ Being visible feels risky — like I'm one poorly-timed comment away from being completely exposed.

☐ I can celebrate other people's wins effortlessly. Accepting my own feels like bragging.

Spoiler: The confidence doesn't come first. Keep reading.

The Myth of Ready

Here's what no one tells you about confidence: it doesn't come before the action. It comes after.

We've been taught otherwise. We've been told — explicitly and implicitly — that confidence is a prerequisite. That you need to *feel* ready before you step forward. That the bold move comes after the bold feeling. That somewhere, on the other side of enough preparation, enough credentials, enough evidence that you know what you're doing, you'll finally feel the thing that gives you permission to act.

So you wait.

You take another course. Earn another certification. Read another book. Revise the plan one more time. You tell yourself you're preparing, but what you're actually doing is building a case — not for your audience or your employer or your client, but for yourself. Collecting proof that you belong, because the feeling of belonging hasn't shown up on its own.

Meanwhile, the man in the next office applies for the job with half your qualifications and doesn't think twice about it. He doesn't feel ready either. He just doesn't think readiness is required.

The confidence gap isn't about ability. It's about permission — who gets it automatically, and who has to earn it one credential at a time.

Good Girls earn. They prepare. They wait.

And the waiting becomes its own kind of hiding.

The Deflection

I have purple hair.

I'm saying that upfront because it matters. Not the color itself — although I love it — but what it represents. I spent years wearing other people's preferences. Adjusting. Accommodating. Building a closet that reflected everyone's taste except mine.

That's behind me now.

These days, my style is mine. Deliberately, unapologetically mine. Purple hair. Colorful glasses. Clothes carefully curated from local boutiques and online shops I've spent years discovering. I dress in bold colors and interesting cuts because that's who I am — the woman I spent a long time burying and a long time finding again.

You'd think, given all that reclamation — given the work I've done to come back to myself — that I'd be able to hear a compliment and let it land.

You'd be wrong.

For years, every time someone noticed — the hair, the glasses, the outfit, the whole curated, intentional, hard — won expression of *me* — I deflected.

"Oh, I got it on sale."

"This? It's just something I had in the back of my closet."

"Oh ... thanks?"

That last one — the upward inflection, the question mark where a period should be — might be the most telling. I couldn't even accept gratitude without turning it into uncertainty. As if saying "*thank you, I chose this deliberately because I love it and it's exactly who I am*" would be too much. Too confident. Too visible.

I got better at it. I'm still getting better at it. But I'd be lying if I said the deflection was gone. It still rises — faster than thought, faster than intention — the reflexive minimizing of anything that points a spotlight in my direction and says *you are worth noticing.*

I can coach other women through this pattern in my sleep. I can see it in a client from across my computer screen — the way she shrinks a compliment, credits the team, apologizes for her own excellence. I can name it, hold space for it, help her unravel it.

And then someone tells me they love my glasses and I say, "Oh these? They were buy one, get one."

The Three Faces of Deflection

Here's what I've learned about why we do this — and it's not one thing. It's three things that rotate depending on the day.

Some days, accepting a compliment feels **arrogant**. Like I'm full of myself. Like the appropriate response to being noticed is to make myself smaller, not bigger. Because Good Girls don't brag. Good Girls certainly don't say "*yes, I know, I chose this because I have excellent taste and I look amazing in it".* That would be too much. That would be taking up space that wasn't offered.

Some days, it feels **unsafe**. Like visibility is an invitation for scrutiny. Like the moment I own the compliment — the moment I stand in the spotlight without flinching — someone will find the flaw. The thing I missed. The crack in the armor. Being noticed feels like being exposed, and being exposed feels like the beginning of a correction. Because in my experience, being seen has often been followed by being told I was wrong.

And some days — the hardest days — it feels **fraudulent**. Like I'll be exposed as someone who isn't actually that good. That the purple hair and the bold glasses are costumes of a different kind — a show of confidence that doesn't go all the way to my core. That underneath the curated exterior, I'm still the woman who doesn't know what she's worth without someone else to validate it.

Arrogant. Unsafe. Fraudulent. Three flavors of the same core belief: *I don't get to own this.*

And so the compliment comes, and the deflection fires before I've had time to choose a different response. "On sale." "Back of the closet." "Oh... thanks?"

Every deflection is a tiny act of self-erasure. A tiny disappearance. A moment where the world says *I see you* and I say *please don't.*

Why This Made Sense

Yet again, the training started early. Specifically and deliberately trained, from an age early enough that it stops feeling like training and starts feeling like our personality.

Think about how girls are praised versus boys. Girls are rewarded for being humble, gracious, self-effacing. Don't be a show-off. Don't be bossy. Don't be full of yourself. Your abilities are acceptable. Your acknowledgment of them is not.

Boys are told to own it. Stand tall. Take the win. Be proud. When a boy excels, the message from the world is: feel good about that. When a girl excels, the message is: be careful not to make anyone else feel bad about it.

By adulthood, the pattern is automatic and invisible. A man says 'thank you, I worked really hard on that' and it's called confidence. A woman says the exact same thing and it's called ego. So she learns to soften. To qualify every word out of her mouth. To credit the team, the timing, the lucky circumstances — anything but her own skill. Because her own skill, claimed out loud, makes people uncomfortable. And making people uncomfortable is the one thing she was never supposed to do.

The over-preparation is the other side of the same coin. If you can't feel confident, you can at least feel qualified. So you collect. Degrees, certifications, courses, credentials. Each one a permission slip that promises: now you've earned the right to take up space. Except the earned never comes, because one more qualification just reveals another gap you're convinced you need to fill.

You were never under-qualified. You've been over-conditioned.

The Confidence Reversal

Here's the secret that nobody tells Good Girls:

Confidence doesn't come before the action. It comes after.

William James observed more than a century ago that action and feeling move together — and that if you can't control the feeling, you can control the action. The feeling, he argued, will follow. Neuroscience has since confirmed what he intuited: the brain learns confidence the same way it learns anything else — through repetition, through reward, through doing the thing enough times that the doing itself becomes the evidence.[15,16]

You don't wait until you feel bold to speak up in the meeting. You speak up, and the boldness arrives — sometimes during, sometimes after, sometimes not until the third or fourth time you do it. But it comes. It always comes. Because confidence isn't a feeling. It's what's left behind after you've done the thing you were afraid to do.

Every woman I've coached who was waiting to feel ready discovered the same thing: the readiness was on the other side of the doing. Not before it. Not as a prerequisite. On the other side — waiting for her, like it had been there all along.

The compliment works the same way. You don't wait until you feel worthy to accept it. You accept it — fully, without qualification — and the worthiness follows. Not because the compliment proves anything. But because the act of receiving, without deflecting, without shrinking, without turning it into a question mark, teaches your nervous system something new:

I am allowed to be seen. And it doesn't have to cost me anything.

That's not arrogance. That's not ego. That's a woman who finally stopped apologizing for being worth noticing.

Choose Your Exit

You've been waiting for confidence to arrive like a Door Dash delivery — something that shows up after enough preparation, enough evidence, enough time. But it doesn't work that way.

Confidence isn't what you feel before you act.

It's what you build by acting.

The Quiet Exit

The next time someone pays you a compliment, you don't deflect. You don't minimize. You don't explain where you got it or how much it cost or why it's not a big deal.

You say: "Thank you."

Period. Full stop. No question mark.

You let the compliment land. You let it sit in your body without swatting it away. You resist the urge to make yourself smaller in the face of being seen.

It will feel uncomfortable. That's not a sign you're doing it wrong. It's a sign you're doing it for the first time.

The Bold Exit

And sometimes the exit is stepping forward before you feel ready.

"I'm going to apply for this even though I don't meet every qualification."

"I have something to say in this meeting, and I'm not going to wait to be called on."

"I'm going to own this — my work, my style, my voice — without apologizing for any of it."

You might not feel confident when you say it. That's fine. The confidence will catch up. It always does.

And the next time someone tells you they love your hair, your glasses, your outfit, your work, your book, your life — the next time someone looks at you and says "*I see you, and what I see is remarkable*" — you don't owe them a discount.

You owe yourself the truth: *Yes. I chose this. And I'm worth every bit of it.*

Chapter 12: The Good Girl Who Is the Eldest Daughter

Is This Your Exit?

☐ I've been "the responsible one" for as long as I can remember — and no one asked if I wanted that job.

☐ I don't ask for help. Not because I don't need it — but because needing it feels like failure.

☐ I take on things that aren't mine — not because I want to, but because if I don't, no one will.

☐ I've been called "the strong one" — and I've never once been asked if that was okay with me.

If you're the one everyone leans on — this chapter leans back.

The First Job You Ever Had

The eldest daughter doesn't apply for the role. She's born into it.

There's no interview. No job description. No negotiation of terms. One day you're a child, and the next — so gradually you don't notice the shift — you're the one who's holding things together. The one who sets the example. The one who figures it out, handles it, manages it, absorbs it, so that the rest of the family can function.

It doesn't always start with a dramatic event. Sometimes it's just the quiet math of birth order. You came first, so you lead first. You're older, so you know better. You're capable, so you carry more.

But sometimes it starts with something sharper. A crisis. A shift in the family's center of gravity. A moment where someone else's needs became louder than yours — and yours, by comparison, became invisible. Not because they didn't exist. Because someone else's were more urgent. And in that urgency, the family recalibrated. The attention flowed toward the crisis. And you — the eldest, the capable one, the one who could handle it — were expected to understand.

And you did understand. You always understood.

The Daughter Who Understood

I'm the eldest.

I have a younger sister, and when we were growing up, the family's attention shifted toward her in a way that was understandable and permanent. She needed more. Not because she demanded it — but because life demanded it on her behalf.

When my sister was 13, she had a major seizure. The kind that stops the room — terrifying and completely without warning. What followed was years of testing. Appointments. Scans. Constant fear. The slow, exhausting process of arriving at a diagnosis: epilepsy.

It was a frightening time for all of us. I know my parents were stressed. I know they were scared. I know they were doing the best they could with a situation that had no playbook.

But their entire focus became my sister. Understandably. Necessarily. And in the reorientation of the family around her needs, mine didn't just take a back seat. They disappeared from the car entirely.

My sister got softer rules. More patience. More latitude. Not because my parents were being unfair — but because the circumstances had changed. She was fragile. I was not. She needed protection. I needed to understand.

And I did understand. I understood so well that I stopped asking for much of anything at all.

When I started acting out — not dramatically, just the ordinary bids for attention that teenagers make when they feel invisible — I wasn't met with curiosity. I was met with anger and punishment. The message was clear: your sister is the one with the real problem. You're the one who should know better.

Even today, my sister's softness and emotional nature are met with tenderness by my mom. She gets held. She gets babied. She gets the gentle response.

I don't usually get that option. I never did.

The Bed I Made

When my first marriage fell apart, I did the hardest thing I'd ever done. I left — not for myself, but for the safety of my daughter.

My parents helped. They paid for the attorney. They gave us a place to stay. They showed up in ways that were tangible, practical, and measurable.

But the emotional support — the kind I actually needed, the kind that says *what happened to you matters, and we're here for the part that hurts* — came with conditions. Came with reminders.

You made your bed. Now you have to lie in it.

I'm so disappointed in you.

They helped me leave. But they didn't help me heal. And the message underneath the disappointment was one I'd been hearing my whole life: *you should have handled this better. You should have known. You shouldn't need us for this.*

I didn't ask for help with the abuse. I wouldn't have known how. The eldest daughter doesn't ask — because asking means admitting she can't handle it, and handling it is the only thing that makes her valuable.

So I handled it. The way I'd always handled everything. Quietly. Competently. Alone.

"The Glue"

The eldest daughter pattern didn't stay in my family. It followed me everywhere.

Into my career. Into my friendships. Into my marriage. Into every room I've ever entered where something needed doing and no one else was stepping up.

At work, I became the person who did the things no one else wanted to do — not because they were beneath anyone, but because I *could*, and being capable was the only currency I trusted. I got the coffee. I took the notes. I tracked down rare auto parts for projects that had nothing to do with my job description.

Once, I compiled a list of my boss's ex-wife's medications — organized, formatted, dropped into a PowerPoint — for his divorce attorney. That wasn't in my job description. It wasn't in anyone's job description. But it needed doing, and I was the eldest daughter, and the eldest daughter doesn't ask *why me?* She asks *what format do you need it in?*

I've been called "the glue" more times than I can count. At work. In my family. In friendships. It's always offered as a compliment — *you're the one who holds everything together, we don't know what we'd do without you.*

I hate it.

I hate it because "the glue" isn't a person. It's a function. It's what you call someone whose entire value lives in what they provide — in their usefulness, their reliability, their willingness to do the thing no one else will do. "The glue" doesn't get to fall apart. "The glue" doesn't get to need things. "The glue" doesn't get to say *actually, I can't hold this right now* — because the moment "the glue" stops holding, everything it's attached to comes undone.

It's not a compliment.

Why the Eldest Daughter Can't Ask

Let's be clear about something: this isn't stubbornness. It's not pride. It's not a personality flaw you can coach yourself out of with the right morning routine.

It's architecture.

When you spend your entire childhood learning that your value comes from what you hold together — the family, the classroom, the team, the vibe — asking for help doesn't just feel uncomfortable. It feels like structural failure. Like the building admitting it can't bear the weight. And buildings don't get to do that. They provide the support. They don't request it.

The eldest daughter learns early that need is a liability. That vulnerability is a disruption. That everyone around her is already stretched — by the sibling who needs more, by the parent who's overwhelmed, by the household that only runs because *she's* running — and adding her own needs to the pile would be selfish. Ungrateful. Too much.

So she stops needing. Or more accurately, she stops *showing* need. The needs don't disappear. They just go underground — the same place her anger went, the same place her wants went, the same place everything went that didn't fit the role.

The role that nobody asked her if she wanted.

The Cost of Being Needed

There's a particular loneliness that belongs to the eldest daughter.

It's not the loneliness of isolation. She's surrounded by people. People who call her first when things go wrong. People who lean on her, rely on her, assume she's fine because she's always been fine. People who love her — genuinely love her — and have no idea that their love has always come with an unspoken condition: *keep holding.*

The loneliness is this: everyone knows they can count on her. And she doesn't know if she can count on anyone.

Not because the people in her life are incapable. But because she's never tested it. She's never let herself need something badly enough, visibly enough, that someone else had to step in. She's never let the ball drop to see who would pick it up — because the idea of the ball dropping is more terrifying than the weight of carrying it forever.

So she keeps carrying. And the people around her keep letting her. Not out of malice — out of habit. Out of the comfort of a system that works, as long as she doesn't stop working.

The eldest daughter's tragedy isn't that she's unloved. It's that she's loved for a role she never chose — and she's terrified that without the role, the love won't hold.

Why That Made Sense

The eldest daughter doesn't choose her role any more than she chooses her birth order. She inherits it — from a family system that needed someone to hold it together, and from a culture that handed that job to the most capable girl in the room without asking if she wanted it.

Research on family systems tells us that children adapt to the emotional needs of their environment.[17] When a family is under stress — illness, financial pressure, a parent's mental health, a sibling's greater need — children reorganize around the crisis. The eldest, already primed by birth order to lead and model, almost always absorbs the most. She becomes the one who understands, who adjusts, who asks for less so that others can have more.

It gets reinforced at every turn. She's praised for being responsible. Trusted with more. Held to a higher standard — not because anyone is being cruel, but because she keeps proving she can handle it. And every time she handles it, the expectation grows. The role calcifies. What started as an adaptation becomes an identity.

By adulthood, she doesn't know how to be anything else. Not because she lacks imagination — but because the role is the only version of herself that has ever been consistently rewarded. Needing things, asking for things, falling apart — those were never options that got reinforced. So she stopped reaching for them.

That's not a character flaw. That's a family system doing exactly what family systems do: finding equilibrium, however unevenly the weight gets distributed.

The problem is she's been carrying her share — and everyone else's — for so long that she's forgotten what it feels like to put it down.

Choose Your Exit

You didn't become the eldest daughter because something was wrong with you. You became her because the family needed someone to hold it together, and you were there. You were first. You were capable. And you rose to it — because that's what eldest daughters do.

But you are not "the glue." You are a person. And people get to need things. People get to fall apart. People get to say *I can't hold this right now* without the entire structure collapsing.

If it does collapse — that was never your building to hold up in the first place.

The Quiet Exit

You notice the urge to volunteer, to manage, to step in before anyone else has a chance to. You pause.

You let someone else figure it out. You let the gap exist without filling it. You sit with the discomfort of not being needed for five minutes and notice that the world doesn't end.

You practice the smallest possible act of need: asking for something. Not apologizing for it. Not minimizing it. Just asking — and letting someone else hold it for once.

The Bold Exit

And sometimes the exit is saying what the eldest daughter has never been allowed to say.

"I need help. Not the logistical kind. The real kind."

"I've been 'the glue' for a long time, and I'm tired of holding everything together."

"I love this family. But I can't keep being the one who carries it — and

I need you to see what that's been costing me."

People will be surprised. Some will be uncomfortable. A few might not know what to do — because you've never needed anything from them before and the reversal will feel unfamiliar.

Let it be unfamiliar. You've been familiar — reliable, steady, the one who handles it — for long enough.

You're allowed to set it down. Even the eldest daughter gets to rest.

Chapter 13: The Good Girl Who Earns Her Joy

Is This Your Exit?

☐ When someone asks what I do for fun, I have to think about it longer than I'd like to admit.

☐ Most of my joy is attached to other people — and I'm genuinely not sure what I enjoy on my own.

☐ I know how to be present for everyone else's happiness. I'm less practiced at my own.

☐ The idea of doing something purely because it brings me joy feels almost … irresponsible.

You don't have to earn this chapter. Just read it.

The Chapter I Almost Couldn't Write

I need to tell you something.

I've written 12 chapters about Good Girl patterns. I've named the shrinking, the performing, the hustle, the silence, the anger, the disappearing. I've told you my stories — the hard ones, the embarrassing ones, the ones that cost me something to put on the page. I've offered frameworks and exits and bold declarations about reclaiming your voice and trusting yourself.

And this chapter — the one about joy — is the one that almost broke me.

Not because I don't understand it. I understand it perfectly. I coach women through it. I can see the pattern in a client from across a Zoom screen — the way she deflects pleasure, justifies rest, earns every good thing instead of simply receiving it. I can name it, hold space for it, help her unravel it.

But when I turned the mirror around and asked myself the question this chapter demands — *What brings you joy that has nothing to do with being useful to someone else?* — I didn't have a clean answer.

I had answers. Just not the ones I expected.

I love spending time with my granddaughter, Flora. Watching her discover the world with that four-year-old mix of wonder and stubbornness fills something in me that I can't describe.

I love a good bottle of wine shared with JP on a quiet evening. The kind of night where neither of us has anywhere to be, where the conversation is easy, and the silence between sentences is comfortable and cozy.

I love a really nice dinner out. The kind where someone else handles the details and I just get to be present (for the record, this rarely happens).

I love books. I love clothes — the hunt for the perfect piece from a boutique I've been stalking online for weeks. I love reality TV, unapologetically, even though admitting that in a book about personal growth feels like it should come with some sort of disclaimer.

But here's what I noticed when I listed all of that: almost every joy on my list includes someone else.

Flora. JP. A dinner companion. A shared bottle of wine.

The joys that are mine alone — the books, the clothes, the guilty, silly television — I almost didn't mention. Because they felt too small. Maybe even a little embarrassing. Not worthy of a chapter about choosing joy.

And that right there? That's the whole pattern.

Why Joy Feels Selfish

Good Girls don't choose joy. They earn it.

Joy is the reward at the end of the to-do list — except the to- do list never ends. So the joy never arrives. Or it arrives with conditions attached: you can enjoy this after the house is clean. After the emails are answered. After everyone else has what they need. You can sit down when you've earned the right to sit down. You can do the thing you love when there's nothing more useful left to do.

And if you do choose joy — if you take the afternoon, buy the dress, watch three episodes of something spectacularly trashy while the laundry sits in the dryer — the guilt is immediate. Automatic. A voice that says: you should be doing something. You should be helping someone. You should be useful right now.

That voice isn't your conscience. It's your conditioning.

It's every lesson you ever absorbed about what makes a woman valuable: productivity, selflessness, service. It's the eldest daughter who was never allowed to stop. It's the hustler who only rests when she collapses. It's every gold star you earned for giving more than you had.

Joy that serves no one else and produces nothing measurable? That's not just unfamiliar. For a lot of us, it feels actively wrong.

Which is exactly why its the hardest exit in this book.

And exactly why it matters so much.

The Joy That Includes Others

Here's where I'm supposed to tell you that real joy is solo. That the goal is a woman alone on a mountaintop, needing no one, perfectly self-contained in her own bliss.

I'm not going to tell you that. Because it's not true for everyone — and it wouldn't be honest.

Some of my deepest joys include other people. And I spent a long time thinking that was a problem. That if my joy was connected to Flora or JP or a shared dinner, it somehow didn't count. That it was just another version of the Good Girl — still oriented outward, still dependent, still finding her value in connection instead of building it alone.

But here's what I've come to understand — slowly, imperfectly, and not without a fight:

There's a difference between joy that includes others and joy that exists *for* others.

Joy that exists for others is performative. It's the dinner party you threw because you felt like you should get to know your neighbors. The vacation you planned around everyone else's preferences. That's not joy. That's acts of service pretending to be joy.

Joy that includes others is something else entirely. It's Flora climbing into my lap because she wants to, not because I earned it. It's JP and I sharing wine because we *choose* each other's company, not because I'm managing his emotional experience. It's a dinner out where I'm not tracking whether everyone else is having a good time — I'm just having one myself.

The difference isn't who's in the room. It's whether *you're* in the room. Whether you're present as yourself — not as the host, the manager, "the glue," the emotional thermostat — but as a woman who is allowed to enjoy this moment without earning it, justifying it, or feeling guilty about it.

I spent years being in rooms full of people and not being present at all. I was too busy holding, tracking, managing, absorbing. The joy was happening around me, and I was its stage manager.

The exit isn't learning to enjoy things alone. It's learning to enjoy things *as yourself* — whether you're alone or surrounded by the people you love.

The Small, Unproductive, Unjustifiable Joys

So let me say something again I almost didn't say, because it felt too small to matter:

I love reality TV.

I love it the way you love something that has absolutely no redeeming productive value. Nobody benefits from me watching it. It doesn't make me a better coach. It doesn't advance my career. It doesn't enrich my mind or strengthen my relationships or contribute to the greater good. In any measurable way.

It's just mine. And it feels good. And for a long time, that wasn't enough to justify it.

I love books — the kind I read for pleasure, not research. The kind that don't show up in a social media post about what I'm learning. The kind I read in bed with the door closed because the reading itself is the point.

I love the hunt for clothes. Not the buying — the *hunting*. The scrolling through online boutiques. The finding of the piece that's exactly right. The moment I put something on and it feels like me — like the bold, colorful, purple-haired woman I fought so hard to become — and I don't have to explain it to anyone.

These aren't grand joys. They're not Instagram-worthy. They don't come with transformation stories or breakthrough moments. They're ordinary, imperfect, private pleasures that exist for no reason other than the fact that they make me happy.

And I'm learning — slowly, daily, with more guilt than I'd like to admit — that *making me happy* is a good enough reason.

Me First

I need to address the phrase that sits at the center of this chapter, because it's the one that makes every Good Girl flinch.

Me first.

Two words. Simple. And almost impossible to say without the guilt rising up like a reflex.

Because "me first" sounds selfish. It sounds like you're cutting in line. It sounds like you're saying *my needs matter more than yours* — and the Good Girl has spent her entire life making sure she never, ever communicates that message.

But "me first" doesn't mean "you don't matter."

It means *I matter too. And I've been going last for so long that I've forgotten I was ever in the line at all.*

Me first is eating before you feed everyone else — not instead of feeding them, but before. Because you can't nourish anyone from an empty place, and you've been running on fumes for years.

Me first is choosing the restaurant you actually want instead of deferring to the group. Wearing the outfit that makes you feel alive instead of the one that makes you invisible. Saying no to the committee, the favor, the extra task — not because you can't do it, but because doing it would cost you something you're no longer willing to pay.

Me first is not a personality overhaul. It's a reordering. A quiet, deliberate insistence that your name belongs on your own list — not at the bottom, after everyone else has been tended to. At the top. Where it should have been all along.

The guilt will come. It always does. Let it come. And then let it pass without obeying it.

You've spent enough of your life going last.

Choose Your Exit

I'm not writing this chapter from the other side. I'm writing it from right here — still in it, still learning, still catching myself earning joy instead of simply letting it happen.

If that makes this chapter different from the others, good. It should be. Because this is the exit that doesn't end. It's not a door you walk through once. It's a choice you make every morning, every evening, every time the guilt whispers *you should be doing something more useful.*

The choice is: *I am doing something useful. I'm living.*

The Quiet Exit

You do one thing today that is just for you. Not for the family. Not for the job. Not for the household or the relationship or the greater good.

Just for you.

Read the book. Watch the show. Buy the dress. Sit in silence for twenty minutes without checking your phone. Take yourself to dinner. Take a walk with no destination.

And when the guilt comes — because it will — you don't fight it. You just notice it, the way you'd notice weather. *Oh, there's the guilt. It's here. And I'm still choosing this.*

The Bold Exit

And sometimes choosing joy is a declaration.

"I'm putting myself first today. Not because I've earned it — because I exist."

"I'm taking the afternoon. The work will be there when I get back."

"This is what I want. That's enough of a reason."

You say it out loud — to your partner, your kids, your colleague, yourself in the mirror on a Tuesday. Not as an apology. Not with a disclaimer attached. Just as a statement of fact about who you are becoming.

Joy is not the reward at the end of the to-do list. It is the evidence that you got out.

Chapter 14: The Good Girl Who Breaks the Pattern

Is This Your Exit?

☐ I can see the patterns now — and I'm exhausted by how long I've been inside them.

☐ I've started making different choices, even small ones — and it feels strange and right at the same time.

☐ I don't want to go back to who I was. I'm just not sure yet who I'm becoming.

☐ I want more than awareness. I want a life that actually feels like mine.

You made it here. Let's finish this.

You've Seen It Now

You can't unsee it.

That's the thing about this work. Once you notice the pattern — the shrinking, the performing, the hustle, the holding, the disappearing — it starts showing up everywhere. In conversations you've had a hundred times. In decisions you made last week. In the reflexive *yes* you offered before you even checked whether you meant it.

You see it in the way you scan a room. In the apology you lead with. In the guilt that rises when you sit still. In the way you carry other people's feelings in your body while your teeth quietly crack under the pressure.

You see it. And once you do, you have a choice.

You can see it and keep going — keep performing, keep shrinking, keep running the same program because it's familiar and safe and you know how to do it in your sleep.

Or you can decide that seeing it is the beginning.

This chapter is about what comes after you see it. The actual path. The framework I use in my coaching practice with women who are exactly where you are right now — awake, aware, and ready to do something about it — finally.

The HERS Experience™

HERS is not a philosophy. It's not a mindset trick. It's not something you read about once and absorb through osmosis.

It's a process. Sequential, intentional, and deeply personal. Four stages that build on each other — each one unlocking the next — until you arrive at something that no Good Girl pattern can touch: an unshakable relationship with yourself.

H — Honesty E — Embodiment R — Reclamation S — Self — Trust

This is how you break the pattern. Not all at once. Not perfectly. But honestly, and for good.

H: Honesty

It starts with the truth. Not the curated version. The real truth — where you are, how you got here, and what you've been carrying that was never yours to hold.

Every chapter in this book has been asking you to get honest.

Honest about the rules you've been following that you never agreed to and don't serve you. Honest about the approval you've been chasing that never actually filled your cup. Honest about the hustle that was never going to prove you were enough — because it was designed to keep you proving forever.

Honesty is the foundation because nothing else works without it. You can't change a pattern you won't name. You can't leave a role you won't admit you've been playing.

And here's what makes this stage hard: the honesty isn't just about what was done to you. It's about what you've been doing to yourself. The ways you've participated in your own shrinking. The moments you chose comfort over truth, belonging over integrity, approval over authenticity.

That's not blame. It's clarity. And clarity is where the exit begins.

Think back to Chapter 1 — the moment you realized you were scanning the room for expectations before checking in with yourself. That was honesty. The flicker of awareness that said, *I've been doing this for years, and I didn't even know it.*

Think about Chapter 6 — the recognition that being "calm under pressure" was actually a performance your body was paying for in cracked teeth and a nervous system running on fumes.

Honesty doesn't require you to have all the answers. It just requires you to stop pretending the questions don't exist.

E: Embodiment

You've been living in your head for years — performing, managing, overthinking. Embodiment brings you back into your body, your instincts, your gut. The part of you that always knew.

The Good Girl lives in her head.

She has to. The head is where the calculations happen — the constant scanning, the reading of rooms, the anticipating of needs, the editing of words before they leave her mouth. It's strategic. It's efficient. And it's completely disconnected from the body that's been keeping score the whole time.

Remember Rachel, in Chapter 5? She tracked every detail of her household — every grocery item, every appointment, every invisible logistical thread — inside her mind. The mental load lived in her head. Meanwhile, her body was exhausted in ways she couldn't even articulate, because she'd stopped listening to it years ago.

Remember the earache in Chapter 3? The body was screaming — *stop, slow down, you are not okay* — and the response was to board another plane.

Remember the parking lot? The shaking hands, the blank windshield, the complete dissociation? That was the body finally overriding the head. Saying: *I'm done waiting for you to listen.*

Embodiment is the practice of coming home to your body. Not as a project to be perfected — not as a problem to be solved with serums and procedures and the endless pursuit of better — but as a source of intelligence.

Your body knows things your mind hasn't caught up to yet. It knows when a room isn't safe. It knows when a yes should have been a no. It knows when you're tired, when you're angry, when you're done. It's been sending signals for years.

Embodiment is learning to hear the signals again. And trusting what they say.

R: Reclamation

This is where you take back what was buried — your voice, your desires, your boundaries, your wild spirit. The parts of you that were told to sit down and be quiet.

Honesty shows you the pattern. Embodiment reconnects you with your body. Reclamation is where you start taking things back. And it can get loud.

Your voice. The one you softened in meetings so you wouldn't be "too much." The one you swallowed at the networking event when a man said something that landed in your solar plexus and you laughed instead of speaking.

Your desires. The ones you buried under obligation and productivity and the endless mental list of what everyone else needed. The ones you forgot to check on because you were too busy checking on everyone else.

Your boundaries. The ones that didn't exist because you were afraid that having them would make you difficult, high — maintenance, excluded. The ones you're now learning to draw — not as walls, but as declarations of what you will and won't carry.

Your anger. The emotion you were never taught how to feel — the one Chapter 10 is about — the one that got redirected into guilt or swallowed into silence. The anger that was always appropriate. That was always yours. That was always trying to protect you.

Your rest. Not earned. Not justified. Not negotiated with guilt. Just taken, because you need it, because you're human, because your husband never once asked permission to play golf on a Saturday and you're done asking permission to exist without producing something.

Reclamation isn't about becoming someone new. It's about retrieving someone old — the version of you that existed before the rules took hold. The girl who didn't mind attention. The one who took up space without self — consciousness. The one who knew what she wanted and said it out loud.

She's still in there.

Reclamation is the act of letting her come back.

S: Self — Trust

The destination isn't confidence. It's something deeper — an unshakable knowing that you are the authority on your own life. No more waiting for permission.

This is where the exit becomes permanent.

Not because you'll never fall back into the pattern — you totally will. The Good Girl is persistent. She'll show up in a meeting when you catch yourself swallowing your opinion. She'll appear at a family dinner when the urge to smooth everything over rises like muscle memory. She'll whisper in your ear at 2 AM that maybe you shouldn't have said that thing, set that boundary, taken that stand.

She'll come back. She always does.

But Self-Trust means you'll recognize her when she shows up. And you'll choose differently anyway.

Self-Trust isn't confidence — not in the way the world sells it. It's not about feeling bold or fearless or certain. It's about knowing that even when you don't feel those things, you can still act from your own authority. You can still choose what's true over what's comfortable. You can still honor your own voice, even when it shakes.

Self-Trust is the moment you stop waiting — for permission, for validation, for someone else to tell you that your instincts are right. It's the moment you realize that the whisper you've been hearing this whole time — the one that said *something needs to change* — was never wrong. Was never selfish. Was always the truest part of you.

You are the authority on your own life.

You always were.

You just forgot — because the world spent a very long time teaching you to trust everyone else's voice above your own.

HERS is how you come back. Not to a new version of yourself. To the real one.

The Body Already Knows: A Note on Menopause

Your body already has its own exit strategy. HERS is the conscious version of what it's already trying to do.

Here's what I mean.

The culture frames menopause as a loss. A decline. The end of fertility, the end of youth, the end of relevance. The beauty industry sees it as a market opportunity — a new set of problems to sell solutions for. The medical establishment treats it as a condition to be managed.

But ask women who've actually gone through it, and a different story emerges.

Many women on the other side of menopause describe something unexpected: freedom. Not the dramatic, cinematic kind. The quiet, cellular kind. A shift in how they move through the world. Less apologizing. Less performing. Less tolerating what they used to swallow without question.

This isn't coincidental. The hormonal shifts of menopause — particularly the decline in estrogen and progesterone — alter neurological patterns in ways that researchers are still mapping. What many women report, anecdotally and in clinical settings, is that the conditioning that kept them compliant for decades begins to loosen.[18]

The women I work with in midlife often describe it the same way: *I woke up one day and just stopped caring. Not in an ugly way. In a liberated way.* The performance that used to feel mandatory suddenly felt optional. The approval that used to feel essential suddenly felt irrelevant. The patterns that had run the show for 30 or 40 years suddenly lost their grip.

This is not a breakdown. This is a biological reclamation.

What HERS offers is the conscious version of what menopause is already doing chemically. Your body is leaving the Good Girl behind. HERS helps the rest of you catch up — your mind, your habits, your relationships, your identity.

And if you're not in menopause yet — if you're in your twenties or thirties or early forties reading this — you don't have to wait for your hormones to give you permission. That's the whole point.

You can start now. The exit doesn't have an age requirement.

Where Are You in Your Exit?

If this book has done its work, you're somewhere in the HERS journey right now. Maybe you're deep in Honesty — finally naming the patterns you've been living inside. Maybe you're at the edge of Embodiment — starting to listen to your body after years of overriding it. Maybe you're already in Reclamation — taking back your voice, your time, your right to exist without performing.

Maybe you're closer to Self-Trust than you think.

Wherever you are, I want you to know: there's no right pace. There's no gold star for getting through HERS faster. (That would be very Good Girl of you, and we both know it.)

If you want to find out where you are, I've created something for that. The Good Girl Score is a short quiz designed to identify exactly where you are in your own exit journey — which patterns are still running the show, which ones you've already started to interrupt, and where your next step lives. You can take it at www.thegoodgirlexit.com.

It's not a test. There's no passing or failing.

It's a mirror. The same kind you've been looking into throughout this book.

Choose Your Exit

This is the last time I'll offer you this choice. Not because the choosing ends here — but because from this point on, you won't need me to frame it.

The Quiet Exit

You close this book and carry it with you — not on your nightstand, but in your body. In the pause before you volunteer. In the breath before you apologize. In the moment you choose what's true over what's expected.

Nobody needs to know. The quiet exit is between you and yourself. And it's enough.

The Bold Exit

You close this book and you act. You have the conversation. You draw the boundary. You leave the job, the room, the relationship, the pattern that has been costing you more than it's giving.

You name it. Out loud. To someone who needs to hear it — even if that someone is you.

Before You Go: Your Exit in the Age of AI

If you've made it this far, you've done something really important.

You've looked at the patterns — the shrinking, the performing, the hustling, the holding, the disappearing — and you've started to see them for what they are. Not who you are. What you learned.

That alone changes things.

But I'd be doing you a disservice if I didn't name what you're walking back into. Because the world didn't pause while you were reading this book. If anything, it sped up.

We are living through the fastest technological shift in human h istory.[19] Artificial intelligence is reshaping how we work, how we communicate, how we create, how we're seen, and how we see ourselves. And for women — particularly women who are already navigating the patterns in this book — AI introduces a new layer of pressure that deserves a clear-eyed look.

Not a panicked one. An honest one.

Here's what I want you to notice:

The beauty standard just went digital — and it's no longer human.

AI can generate faces that don't exist. Flawless, symmetrical, ageless faces that set a benchmark no living woman can meet — because they were never alive to begin with. Filters powered by AI smooth your skin, reshape your jaw, enlarge your eyes in real time. The woman you're comparing yourself to on social media may not be a woman at all. She may be an agent's idea of what a woman should look like.

If Chapter 7 made you question who set the beauty standard, AI should make you question whether the standard is even real anymore.

The hustle just got a new competitor.

AI can write faster than you. It can analyze faster, summarize faster, produce faster. And if you're a Good Girl who already measures her worth in output — who already believes she has to be the hardest worker in the room to justify her seat — this feels like a threat. The instinct is to work *more*, to prove you're still valuable, to outpace the machine.

But here's the truth: your productivity is real. Your worth is not contingent on it. Those are two different things — and the Good Girl has been confusing them her whole life.

The mental load didn't disappear. It got a new interface.

AI promises to simplify your life — meal planning apps, automated grocery lists, smart calendars, digital assistants that manage your family's schedule. And yet, someone still has to set it all up. Someone still has to choose the app, input the preferences, troubleshoot when it breaks, and teach everyone else in the house how to use it.

Three guesses who that someone is.

The mental load doesn't vanish because the tools get smarter. It just shape shifts. And if you're not paying attention, you'll find yourself managing the AI that was supposed to manage your life.

Your voice, your likeness, your work — all of it can be replicated.

AI can clone your voice. It can generate your image. It can produce content in your style without your permission. For women who already struggle with visibility — who already wonder whether their contributions will be credited, whether their ideas will be heard, whether their presence matters — this is not a neutral development.

The Good Girl who learned to disappear now lives in a world where technology can make her disappear faster, more completely, and without her consent.

The algorithm decides who gets seen.

AI screens resumes. AI curates dating profiles. AI determines which social media posts reach an audience and which ones vanish into the void. The Good Girl who waits to be chosen is now waiting to be chosen by a system she can't read, can't charm, and can't people-please into liking her.

The old playbook — be agreeable, be attractive, be easy to work with — doesn't work on an algorithm. Which might actually be the most liberating thing about this whole shift.

So what do you do with all of this?

You do exactly what this book has been asking you to do all along.

You stay honest — with yourself about what you're feeling, what you're consuming, and what you're allowing to define your worth.

You stay embodied — in your actual body, your actual face, your actual life, not the filtered, optimized, algorithmically perfected version of it.

You reclaim what's yours — your voice, your time, your attention, your right to exist as a full human being in a world that increasingly wants to reduce you to data points.

And you trust yourself — more than the feed, more than the filter, more than the machine that promises to make your life easier if you'd just hand over a little more of yourself.

AI isn't the enemy. But it is an amplifier. It will amplify the patterns you've already been living — the comparison, the hustle, the invisibility, the performance — unless you've done the work to interrupt them.

And you have.

That's what this book was for. Not to make you afraid of what's coming. But to make sure that when it arrives, you meet it as yourself.

Not the Good Girl.

You.

Your exit was never about leaving the world behind. It was about stopping long enough to decide how you want to move through it — on your terms, in your voice, with your eyes wide open.

The world will keep changing. Technology will keep advancing. The pressures will keep shape shifting.

But you don't have to shape shift with them.

You just have to keep choosing — honestly, deliberately, and without apology — who you want to be.

Congratulations. You're officially harder to manage.

Your exit doesn't end here. Take the Good Girl Score at quiz.thegoodgirlexit.com to see what's next.

Or come find your people at thegoodgirlexit.substack.com. I've been saving you a seat.

Sources

Sources

1. Murthy, V.H. (2023). *Our epidemic of loneliness and isolation: The U.S. Surgeon General's advisory on the healing effects of social connection and community.* U.S. Department of Health and Human Services. https://www.hhs.gov/sites/default/files/surgeon-general-social-connection-advisory.pdf

2. Lieberman, M. D. (2013). *Social: Why our brains are wired to connect.* Crown Publishers.

3. National Sleep Foundation. (2022, March 13). *Screen use disrupts precious sleep time.* https://www.thensf.org/screen-use-disrupts-precious-sleep-time/

4. Daminger, A. (2019). The cognitive dimension of household labour. *American Sociological Review, 84*(4), 609–633.

5. Statista. (2025). *Beauty & personal care — worldwide.* https://www.statista.com/outlook/cmo/beauty-personal-care/worldwide

6. Market.us. (2024). *Anti-aging market size, share, growth.* https://market.us/report/global-anti-aging-market/

7. New Beauty. (2022, March 10). *This is the generation most worried about aging.* https://www.newbeauty.com/millennials-reportedly-worry-more-about-aging-than-their-moms-or-grandmothers/

8. Chamorro-Premuzic, T. (2019, October 31). *Attractive people get unfair advantages at work. AI can help.* Harvard Business Review. https://hbr.org/2019/10/attractive-people-get-unfair-advantages-at-work-ai-can-help

9. SkinStore.com. (2017, April 28). *Women spend $200K on makeup in a lifetime* [Survey reported by TODAY]. NBC Universal. https://www.today.com/style/women-spend-200k-makeup-lifetime-skinstore-com-survey-t109772

10. Gettysburg College. (n.d.). *One third of your life is spent at work.* https://www.gettysburg.edu/news/stories?id=79db7b34-630c-4f49-ad32-4ab9ea48e72b

11. Rice, C. (2014, April 22). *Anecdata, or how McKinsey's story became Sheryl Sandberg's fact.* https://curt-rice.com/2014/04/22/what-happens-when-underqualified-women-apply-for-jobs-and-why-sheryl-sandberg-and-mckinsey-wrongly-think-we-dont-know/

12. Coffman, K.B., Collis, M. R., & Kulkarni, L. (2024). *Whether to apply.* Harvard Business School. https://www.library.hbs.edu/working-knowledge/breaking-through-the-self-doubt-that-keeps-talented-women-from-leading

13. Chaplin, T.M., & Aldao, A. (2013). Gender differences in emotion expression in children: A meta-analytic review. *Psychological Bulletin, 139*(4), 735–765.

14. van der Kolk, B. A. (2014). *The body keeps the score: Brain, mind, and body in the healing of trauma*. Viking.

15. James, W. (1892). *Psychology: The briefer course*. Henry Holt and Company.

16. Robertson, I. (as cited in Robson, D., 2025, August 2). Confidence is a trick that can be taught. *BBC Science Focus*. https://www.sciencefocus.com/wellbeing/confidence-trick-can-be-taught

17. Bowen, M. (1978). *Family therapy in clinical practice*. Jason Aronson.

18. Mosconi, L., et al. (2021). Menopause impacts human brain structure, connectivity, energy metabolism, and amyloid-beta deposition. *Scientific Reports, 11*, 10867. https://www.nature.com/articles/s41598-021-90084-y

19. Roser, M., Ritchie, H., & Mathieu, E. (2023). *Technological change*. Our World in Data. https://ourworldindata.org/technological-change

www.ingramcontent.com/pod-product-compliance
Lightning Source LLC
LaVergne TN
LVHW090935150826
845672LV00006B/1516

* 9 7 9 8 2 3 4 0 5 9 4 4 4 *